MPACT 1620

iten
g James
d king
mento
ago to
God
ck, and
into a
c fur=
ncte;
nances,
thought
unto
witnes
Cap=
eraigne
eighteenth

IN the Name of God, Amen. [...] whose Names are under-written, the Loyal Subjects of our dread Soveraign Lord King James, by the grace of God of Great Britain, France and Ireland, King, Defender of the Faith, &c. Having undertaken for the glory of God, and advancement of the Christian Faith, and the Honour of our King and Countrey, a Voyage to plant the first Colony in the Northern parts of Virginia; Do by these Presents solemnly and mutually, in the presence of God and one another, Covenant and Combine our selves together into a Civil Body Politick, for our better ordering and preservation, and furtherance of the ends aforesaid: and by virtue hereof do enact, constitute and frame such just and equal Laws, Ordinances, Acts, Constitutions and Officers, from time to time, as shall be thought most meet and convenient for the general good of the Colony; unto which we promise all due submission and obedience. In witness whereof we have hereunto subscribed our Names at Cape Cod, the eleventh of November, in the Reign of our Soveraign Lord King James, of England, France and Ireland the eighteenth, and of Scotland the fifty fourth, Anno Dom. 1620.

This was the first Foundation of the Government of Plimouth.

John Carver.	Samuel Fuller.	Edward Tilly.
William Bradford.	Christopher Martin.	John Tilly.
Edward Winslow.	William Mullins.	Francis Cook.
William Brewster.	William White.	Thomas Rogers.
Isaac Allerton.	Richard Warren.	Thomas Tinker.
Miles Standish.	John Howland.	John Ridgdale.
John Alden.	Steven Hopkins.	Edward Fuller.
John Turner.	Digery Priest.	Richard Clark.
Francis Eaton.	Thomas Williams.	Richard Gardiner.
James Chilton.	Gilbert Winslow.	John Allerton.
John Craxton.	Edmond Margeson.	Thomas English.
John Billington.	Peter Brown.	Edward Doten.
Joses Fletcher.	Richard Bitteridge.	Edward Liester.
John Goodman.	George Soule.	

COMPACT

The "Compact", with the signers, as first printed in "Morton's Memorial" at Cambridge, Mass., in 1669, an official publication of the Plymouth Colony. The order of signing the original manuscript is not known.

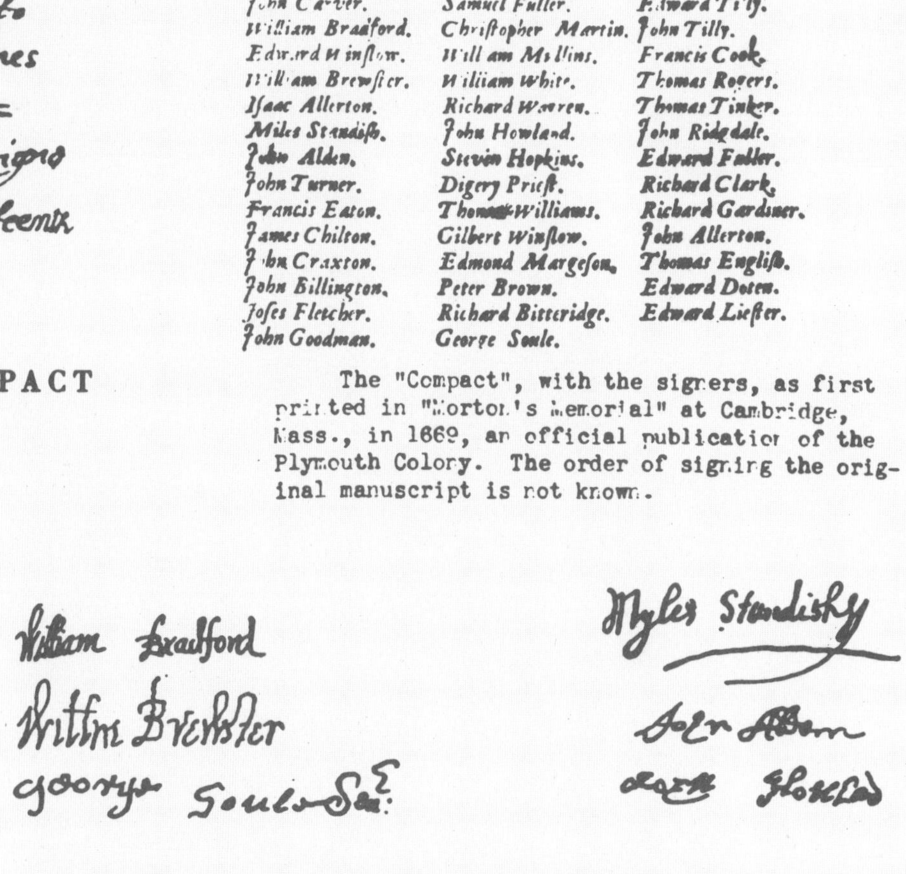

OF SOME OF THE SIGNERS

The
MAYFLOWER
MIRACLE

The
MAYFLOWER MIRACLE

The Pilgrims' Own Story of the Founding of America

JONATHAN KING

DAVID & CHARLES
Newton Abbot   London

*'Friend, if ever we make a
plantation, God works a mirakle;
especially considering how scante
we shall be of victualls, and most
of all ununited amongst our
selves, & devoyd of good tutors &
regiment'*

Robert Cushman
Pilgrim leader
17 August 1620

A P.I.C. CO-VENTURE

British Library Cataloguing in Publication Data

King, Jonathan, *1942-*
  The Mayflower miracle: the pilgrim's
  own story of the founding of America.
  1. Pilgrims (New Plymouth colony)
  I. Title
  973.2′2   F68

ISBN 0-7153-9013-9

First published
by David & Charles 1987

© Jonathan King 1987

Printed in Hong Kong
for David & Charles plc
Brunel House
Newton Abbot   Devon

Contents

Introduction:
The Vine of Israel

*'Thus out of smalle beginings greater
things have been produced by his hand
that made all things of nothing, and
gives being to all things that are; and as
one small candle may light a thousand,
so the light here kindled hath shone to
many, yea in some sorte to our whole
nation; let the glorious name of Jehova
have all the praise.'*

William Bradford

The Pilgrim story is an astonishing saga of heroic men and women battling against the elements to realize an impossible dream.

If a modern writer presented the story as a novel he may have difficulty finding a publisher, as the epic drama seems inconceivable. But the adventures of this brave little band struggling towards their noble goal were all true. As a tale it is as dramatic as Homer's mythical Ulysses fighting his way back home from Troy to Ithaca; and as a story it is more important, because the story of the miracle of the Pilgrims' settlement is also the story of the miracle of America.

When the Pilgrims founded their settlement at Plymouth in 1620, they planted seeds from which modern America grew. The character of that original settlement, more than anything else, has influenced the fundamental character of Americans and their way of life. Consequently the story of the Pilgrims is of great significance to every modern American.

The period in which the Pilgrims lived was oppressive. People were burnt at the stake for saying things that upset the church or state authorities. There was no freedom of religion. People died for believing in the wrong God. In fact the Spanish Inquisition was developed to hunt down and torture people who were suspected of not having the right religious beliefs. The Roman Catholic church dominated the world and the armies of Europe enforced its rules and regulations. The Thirty Years War tore Europe apart during the period as Catholics and Protestants fought over the fundamental questions of religion.

For decades it was an uncertain and violent world as the Spanish,

Dutch and English fought over colonial possessions claiming different parts of America. Explorers like Sir Walter Ralegh were in favor one moment and then beheaded the next. The English King Henry VIII had broken with the Roman Catholic Church, creating the Church of England to facilitate his divorce and the seeds of bitter religious strife began to take root.

The England that the Pilgrims left was an England undergoing great change and upheaval. During the first quarter of the seventeenth century James I authorized the new Bible; Shakespeare was writing provocative plays like *Hamlet* portraying the problems of kings and princes. Ben Jonson was irritating people with his satirical essays; Milton was elevating people's thoughts with such poetic works as *Paradise Lost*, John Donne was seducing his ladies with love poems and Francis Bacon was startling society with his scientific essays and lectures.

The Pilgrims were not the first to sail the Atlantic Ocean for America. Christopher Columbus had achieved this honor in 1492 but they were among the first to settle the continent for the English. Others like Captain John Smith and the settlers of Virginia had explored the east coast from the early seventeenth century. There was plenty of information on the new world. Commercial interests had settled Virginia in 1607 at Jamestown and books had been published extolling the virtues of America as a new world for the brave. Nevertheless it was still a long way and a very risky undertaking.

Escaping from the oppressive English authorities and seeking a land where they could practise their religion in peace, the Pilgrims established the importance of personal principles from the start. By fighting so hard for their religious freedom, they created documents like the 1620 Mayflower Compact and the 1643 New England Confederation and established the important principles of freedom of conscience, freedom of religion, the right to life, liberty and the pursuit of happiness, enshrining the basic concepts and rights of the First Amendment of the Constitution of the United States.

The Pilgrims brought with them to the new land such concepts as freedom of opinion, right to dissent, the principle of fair and open debate, the practise of electing governments democratically and the idea of having a written document establishing the rules and regulations of government. The Mayflower Compact in time influenced the Constitution of the United States. The Pilgrims also created a new code of morality and behavior. They asserted the rights of people against the British Crown, established the concept of the common good, of the general will of the people, of the greatest happiness of the greatest number and, through their disciplined leadership, laid the basis for government by the people, for the people and of the people.

Despite the religious ideals the Pilgrim settlement was established on a commercial footing from the start. The Plymouth Plantation was an investment arrangement, between London speculators who ventured capital and their work force — the Pilgrims. They introduced to America the spirit of free enterprise through their conscious decision to abandon their early communal system in favor of private enterprise, as they found the latter far more efficient.

Their religious inspiration enabled them to succeed, where others had failed and, while hundreds of commercial settlers were massacred in Virginia, forcing them to abandon their settlements, the Pilgrims survived. Above all else, of course, the Pilgrims considered themselves saints on a divine mission, attempting to create a heaven on earth. They saw themselves as the chosen people, successors to the Israelites who, like the vine of Israel, had been plucked by the hand of God, transported across the seas and transplanted in the promised land. Motivated by the purist religious ideals, they founded a religious settlement which in turn laid the basis for a strong religious foundation for the future American nation. As Bradford wrote: 'they knew they were pilgrimes, & looked not much on those things, but lift up their eyes to the heavens, their dearest cuntrie, and quieted their spirits'.

The Pilgrims had the conviction of men on a mission, united by heartfelt convictions and ideas of the mind, that forged them together emotionally and intellectually, giving them a common bond that each of them in turn would gladly have died for. As a result they had a noble sense of purpose, incredible courage and relentless persistence; one hundred and two Pilgrims against one hundred and two obstacles. Bradford related: 'their condition was not ordinarie; their ends were good & honourable; their calling lawfull, & urgente; and therefore they might expecte the blessing of God in their proceding. Yea, though they should loose their lives in this action, yet might they have comforte in the same, and their endeavors would be honourable'.

The Pilgrims paved the way for latter-day emigrants to America; their cause is like the cause symbolized by the Statue of Liberty. They were the forerunners of the political refugees of European wars — from the mid-seventeenth century through to the great exodus of the Jews from Nazi Europe.

Despite the high ideals that did so much to start America off on the right foot, the Pilgrim story is a tale of woe. They were the 'wrong' sort of people to create the settlement and generally made a mess of it. Their religion, which was their greatest asset, ironically was potentially also their greatest enemy. Although it gave them purpose and discipline it encouraged them to delay and dither while praying for guidance and deliberating in religious terms the significance and consequences of everyday matters. This same faith also made them rationalize unbelievable hardships that they should have avoided.

It was a miracle that these simple and disorganized country folk overcame the obstacles that fell in their path. No other group could ever have had so many problems to overcome and no other group could ever have had the tenacity and good fortune to overcome them. Perhaps no other group would ever have been prepared to sacrifice half their number to achieve their ends, either.

The Pilgrims were betrayed all along the way. Even initially, their fellow Englishmen informed on them within their own Parish; they were betrayed by commercial seamen as they tried to cross the Channel while escaping from England to Holland; families were split up with men being forced to leave women and children to the mercy of the angry English authorities; they were discriminated against in Holland, finding it difficult to get good jobs.

The Dutch lifestyle and language undermined their mission; they did not have enough money to pay for the hire of a ship to take them to America. They were exploited by the investors who changed the terms and conditions of the commercial contract that established the basis of the Pilgrim settlement in America, forcing them to give up equity in their own houses and land, in a far greater share of the profits and to work on Sundays. They could not afford to pay the harbor dues in England and had to sell precious supplies to clear the port. The ships they selected were too small; one of them leaked so badly that it had to turn back, even though the leak was probably manufactured by a cunning captain and crew anxious to break an unattractive contract.

The *Mayflower* itself nearly sank in high seas halfway across the Altantic when the ship's main beam collapsed as a result of the stormy weather; one of the Pilgrims was washed overboard; the ship was blown off course and landed in the wrong place; they had arrived in North America far too late in the year and the ground was all covered with snow.

On arrival they realized they had forgotten many important pieces of equipment, such as fish hooks and building tools. The rudder and mast on their little longboat collapsed on the first expedition in the colony. The pilot got lost. They were attacked by Indians moments after they decided to leave their guns on a beach; and almost every time they went out exploring they forgot to take enough food, water or camping equipment. But above all else it was their intellectual approach that delayed progress, for they spent too much time dithering and deliberating on fundamental questions.

It is indeed a tale of woe. Yet the Pilgrims were saved by many miracles. They did find sympathizers to take them from England to Holland; they had inspiring and charismatic leaders; they survived the storms and seasickness on the oceans, they were able to fish John Howland back out of the water when he went overboard; they just happened to have the large iron screw in their possessions that was needed to repair the broken *Mayflower* in mid-Atlantic. Their chance landing at Cape Cod was a blessing in disguise as the resources were abundant; they found supplies of corn ready to eat, within days of arriving, in buried Indian larders; they shot their way out of early Indian attacks and they had the great good fortune to be befriended by civilized Indians such as Samoset and Squanto, who taught them the ways of the New World and how to survive.

There were of course bad eggs in the Pilgrim basket, such as John Billington and Isaac Allerton who were the first betrayers of the common cause, but in general, standards of the Pilgrims were very high.

The events of this story happened a long time ago. Lots of dates and names went missing long ago. This book does not claim to tell the whole truth and nothing but the truth. It does however attempt to portray the truth as closely as possible and although the line is blurred from time to time it is more fact than fiction.

In this book the original dates given by the Pilgrims have been used as the chronology. However it should be remembered that the calendar year in the seventeenth century was different from the modern calendar. Today we start the New Year on 1 January. Then, the Pilgrims started the New Year on 25 March. However, in this book I have taken the liberty of starting the year on 1 January, even though I have used the old dates as the basis for the chronology.

In most cases the direct quotes are taken from Bradford's Journal, *Of Plimoth Plantation*. The accounts given by Winslow which are not in direct quotes, are generally from his Relation, or Journal, published by George Mourt, and which are often referred to as *Mourt's Relation*.

The intention has been to let the Pilgrims tell their own story as much as possible, so I have attempted to minimize comment. At the same time the ancient English is explained to the reader in a popular style that makes it intelligible.

As Bradford's manuscript was lost for so many years, it is important now to bring his writings to the notice of the American public. If, in some cases, a word is totally unintelligible, it has been altered for convenience. These changes include 'the' for 'ye' and 'that' for 'yt'. It should also be noted that there are many inconsistencies in spelling throughout the journal, and that historically, there are also many inconsistencies in the facts presented from various sources.

The book has been written for the man on the street, as this is where the story should be told. There are many excellent scholarly references on the Pilgrims and this is by no means an attempt to supercede any of these books that have gone before.

But in order to understand their story, we have to look at who the Pilgrims were, what principles they held dear, why they chartered the *Mayflower* and, in essence, what it was to be a Pilgrim.

To be a Pilgrim

He who would valiant be
Gainst all disaster,
Let him in constancy
Follow the Master.
There's no discouragement
Shall make him once relent
His first avowed intent
To be a pilgrim.

John Bunyan

There have been many pilgrims over the ages but none have captured the imagination of the world as much as the brave little band who settled America in 1620. Although pilgrims are defined as wanderers who travel to some sacred place as an act of religious devotion, the title has also come to represent those inspired English puritans who crossed the Atlantic Ocean and founded the colony of Plymouth in Massachusetts — the Pilgrim Fathers.

The English tradition of seeking a pure and simple Christian way of life developed over the centuries. These values were initially extolled by English reformer William Langland in his fourteenth-century classic, *The Vision Concerning Pier's The Ploughman*. Inspired by this and other teachings dedicated believers sought religious purification by travelling to Canterbury Cathedral and this pilgrimage was immortalized in Chaucer's fourteenth-century poem *Canterbury Tales*. The progress of these religious zealots from earthly sin to celestial purity was also described in John Bunyan's seventeenth-century classic, *Pilgrim's Progress*, which itself was celebrated in his seventeenth century hymn, *To be a Pilgrim*.

People have sought the promised land since the start of time and many writers have attempted to portray this ideal including Thomas More who wrote *Utopia* in 1516 describing a world in which people lived in perfect harmony and which influenced such idealists as the Pilgrim fathers.

1

Pilgrim Principles The Pilgrims were people of consequence because of their principles. They had a definite set of beliefs that made them who they were and created a framework for their life.

Their official scribe William Bradford summarized their philosophy when he claimed 'their condition was not ordinarie; their ends were good & honourable; their calling lawfull, & urgente; and therefore they might expecte the blessing of God in their proceding. Yea, though they should loose their lives in this action, yet might they have comforte in the same, and their endeavors would be honourable.'

Their spiritual leader, the Reverend John Robinson, also summed up their religious position before the Pilgrims set out on their American mission, when he provided them with a basic five-point statement of pilgrim philosophy explaining why they were better equipped than anyone else to carry out God's work on earth:

1. We veryly beleeve & trust the Lord is with us, unto whom & whose service we have given our selves in many trialls; and that he will graciously prosper our indeavours according to the simplicitie of our harts therin.

2. We are well weaned from the delicate milke of our mother countrie, and enured to the difficulties of a strange and hard land, which yet in a great parte we have by patience overcome.

3. The people are for the body of them, industrious, & frugall, we thinke we may safly say, as any company of people in the world.

4. We are knite togeather as a body in a most stricte & sacred bond and covenante of the Lord, of the violation wherof we make great conscience, and by vertue wherof we doe hould our selves straitly tied to all care of each other good, and of the whole by every one and so mutually.

5. Lastly, it is not with us as with other men, whom small things can discourage, or small discontentments cause to wish them selves at home againe.

Among other things the Pilgrims were non-conformists who believed in freedom of individual conscience; freedom of worship; the right to communicate with God directly and not through intermediaries or church officials; religious tolerance and the simplicity of religious life, taking exception to materialistic exploitation expressed in the manufacture and sale of relics, indulgences and other physical trappings of faith.

Like other puritans they viewed with suspicion the interpretation of the Gospel by the Roman Catholic Church, with its secular trappings and the power claimed and accumulated by the Pope. After King Henry VIII had broken from the Roman Catholic Church, they regarded the subsequent reformation of the church under Queen Elizabeth I as incomplete, and called for its further 'purification' from unscriptural and corrupt forms and ceremonies retained from the unreformed church.

Most puritans advocated this kind of purity of doctrine and practice. They insisted on extreme adherence to biblical principles, and collectively they led a life of consequent austerity. In England many puritans separated from the established church on points of ritual or doctrine, disliking the hierarchy of bishops. Some of these were consequently labelled Separatists; while others who followed the leadership of Elder Brown were called Brownists. There were many such religious factions breaking away from the mainstream English church during this period.

But the Pilgrims were a group unto themselves with strong convictions that drove them away from prejudice and persecution to create a new world across the Atlantic Ocean. They believed that to regain the simplicity of their faith they had to establish a direct covenant with the Lord 'as the Lords free people, joyned them selves', abolishing the hierarchy of bishops with their 'courts, cannons, and ceremonies', their 'popish trash' and their luxurious livings which oppressed the poor.

The Prominent Pilgrims

Of the one hundred and two Pilgrims who set out to colonize America, some achieved more prominence than others. As half of the Pilgrims died in the first winter, many of them did not have time to distinguish themselves. There were however at least ten prominent Pilgrims who emerged as significant characters in the settlement of America.

William Bradford

William Bradford is one of America's forgotten heroes. He was to the Pilgrim period of American history what George Washington was to the glorious War of Independence. Yet he remains an unsung hero.

Bradford was the longest serving leader and official scribe of the Pilgrims expedition to America. He left the most comprehensive and accurate record of the whole event as his Journal traces the story from the start to the finish. From the sailing of the *Speedwell* from the Dutch harbor Delfshaven, Bradford's life is inseparable from the history of the Pilgrim colony.

His journal is the main source of information on this epic event. Although it was lost for many decades it reappeared in time to serve as a basis for this present book. Bradford did not begin to write his history *Of Plimoth Plantation* until about 1630. Even then it was not really written for publication, as he intended the book to be handed down to his family. It was fortunate that this original manuscript survived at all, as after the American War of Independence the journal disappeared and was considered lost for many generations until it reappeared in the nineteenth century in England, among the papers of the Lord Bishop of London. Consequently this epic account was not printed in full until 1856 and was not returned to America until 1897.

Bradford came from a rural family of yeomen, who had for many generations lived in the northern English county of Yorkshire, where many of the hardest workers traditionally lived — people described by many as the 'salt of the earth'. His earliest ancestors lived at Bentley-cum-Arksey (five miles from Austerfield) in Yorkshire from at least 1450. The family moved to Austerfield about forty years prior to William's birth. Having come from a line of well-to-do yeomen, it was expected he would follow in this line.

Bradford was born in 1589 and baptized 19 March 1590 at the little church at Austerfield, three miles north of Scrooby. His father died in 1591, when William was only one year old, leaving the child to be brought up firstly by his grandfather, then his uncles, in nearby Wellingly, a name which in time Bradford was going to transport to Plymouth. Many of his fellow Pilgrims came from a collection of nearby towns, such as Gainsborough, Scrooby, Babworth and Sturton-le-steeple; these lay within a two-mile circle.

Unlike his fellow Pilgrims however Bradford was an exceptional man, with a strictly disciplined intellect and heartfelt emotions, that were grounded on a diligent and comprehensive reading of religious works. Of all the Pilgrims, the title of 'saint' sits most comfortably on his shoulders.

His early religious instruction came from the Geneva Bible and Calvinist manuals, although he devoured any other relevant religious texts that he could lay his hands on. At the age of twelve, he would walk ten miles to Babworth to hear the nonconformist preacher Richard Clifton advocating a puritan approach to religious life. As a result, Bradford quarrelled with his uncles on points of religion. They subsequently gave up on him and he fell then under the influence of the puritan leader, Elder William Brewster, who would in time create the Pilgrim group.

Bradford was inspired to enlist in the band which became a separatist church in 1606. He was among the first to escape the tyranny of England, crossing the Channel to Holland where he became a citizen of Leyden. There, he was working as a weaver by 1613, earning enough money to buy a house on the Achtergracht, which he sold in 1619 before leaving for America.

Bradford married Dorothy May, on 10 December 1613 in Amsterdam. Their only son, John, came to Plymouth later, married and died without issue. Dorothy drowned when she fell overboard soon after arrival in Cape Cod Harbour in 1620. Bradford then married a former member of the Leyden Church, a widow, Alice Southworth, on 14 August 1623. She had arrived on the *Anne* with her two small sons in the July of that year. They had a daughter and two sons, William and Joseph.

Throughout his life Bradford was a competent and popular Governor and was elected as the second Governor of the colony for the first time at the age of thirty two. After this he was elected Governor thirty times and assistant five times. No other administrator did so much to ensure the success of the Pilgrim colony and lay the foundations of America.

Although in 1624 he urged rotation in office, the only times he was not elected Governor were 1633, 1634, 1636, 1638, and 1644 and on those occasions he was elected an assistant. Until 1639 when he was voted £20, he received no salary. Up to 1651 he even had to feed and dine the court of assistants at his own expense during their monthly sessions. He was by example the epitomy of the Pilgrim principles and values.

He regarded the colony as an overseas Congregational Church and conducted it as such whenever possible, although the franchise was never restricted to church members. His government could not be described as truly democratic because in 1623 he declared that the generality were allowed to share in the government 'only in some weighty matters, when we thinke good'. Nevertheless Bradford was always open to debate and new ideas. In practise the Pilgrim rank and file vested almost complete discretionary authority in their Governor.

A man of many talents Bradford was also a fine writer. He expressed himself beautifully with a wide variety of references, both religious and secular, and his words are a joy to read. From the start he had taken notes and had helped Winslow write the 1622 account of the Pilgrim settlement, which was edited by George Mourt, and subsequently referred to as *Mourt's Relation*. This account was the first published story of the beginning and proceedings of the English Plantation settled at Plymouth in New England by certain English adventurers, both merchants and others. It told of their difficult passage, safe arrival, joyful building of, and comfortable planting themselves in, the now well-defended town of New Plymouth, and concluded with stories on several discoveries made by some of these English planters. Bradford's own, and considerably more complete, *Of Plimoth Plantation*, deals with the inception of the colony and its history to 1647.

Bradford was also a self-made man and a thinker; a man of action; a fatherly figure of considerable charm, linguist, farmer, businessman, magistrate, diplomat and most of all a man of God. He lived to the age of sixty eight, dying on 19 May 1657. The old man of the colony by then had seen many changes and sadly came to believe by the end of his life that the direction being taken by his descendants and the younger generation was away from the straight and narrow path. In fact he died believing the God-given glory had departed from the Plymouth Colony.

Edward Winslow
After William Bradford, Edward Winslow was perhaps the most important leader in the Pilgrim group. Apart from Bradford, the main records of the *Mayflower* adventure were in fact written by Edward Winslow in the account known as *Mourt's Relation*.

He was more of a man of the world than Bradford and was just as comfortable in the Royal Courts of England, the primitive colonies of America or on a mission to the West Indies for Oliver Cromwell. As a man of some substance, with a good and wealthy family background,

The Pilgrim leader Edward Winslow. He published all his experiences in London encouraging future settlers to travel to the New World.

his skills were wider as well. Having enjoyed a good education his talents were many and varied. Through his own vast experience he also acquired a useful knowledge of the ways of the world and was a great help to the Pilgrims in their business dealings.

If it had not been for Winslow, we would not have known what any of the Pilgrims looked like, because he is the only Pilgrim whose portrait has survived. This portrait shows his kind and friendly face and reveals that he was a gentleman of some dignity.

Like Bradford, Winslow was a good writer and collaborated with Bradford in the writing of the 1622 book, *Mourt's Relation*, the first book published on the colony. His writing style is professional and he had an excellent eye for detail often noting and recording events missed by Bradford. Together they provide a first class record.

Winslow was baptized on 18 October 1595 at Worcester. He was a descendant of the Winslow family of Kempsey, Worcestershire, where the estate was called 'Kerswell'; so he later called his estate in Plymouth 'Careswell'. His early occupation was recorded as a printer but in 1624 at the age of thirty, he described himself as a yeoman. In 1614, when he was nineteen, he was betrothed in Leyden to Elizabeth Barker. His wife died on 24 March 1621. On 12 May 1621, Edward Winslow married Susanna White, the widow of William White, which Bradford described as the 'first marriage in this place'.

Winslow was elected Governor three times, sharing the position with William Bradford. He performed well in office and the colony progressed under his leadership. Winslow also played a critical role in all the negotiations with the Indians, participating in many meetings, especially those held to establish peace with the great Indian chief, Massasoit.

Following his period of service in the colony, Winslow returned to England where he served the new commonwealth government of the Puritan revolutionary Oliver Cromwell, as a foreign ambassador negotiating new treaties inspired by Cromwell's religious policies in such far-flung outposts as the West Indies. He died in the West Indies of a tropical disease.

Captain Myles Standish

Standish was the heroic soldier in the colony. He was also one of the more colorful figures in the Pilgrim group and, if there was a folk hero among their number, it was Myles Standish, who was affectionately known by those he protected as 'Captain Shrimp'.

Standish was a brave and enterprising soldier who initiated and led many of the exploring parties in the new colony, fearlessly penetrating virgin tracts of untamed land, leading the Pilgrims from one day to the next. It was Standish who defended the Pilgrims against the Indians, repulsing every attack and personally killing the worst of the Indian leaders. It was Standish who trained them in the art of self-protection and taught them that guns were as important in the new land as bibles.

Perhaps surprisingly, little is conclusively known about his early years. He was born around 1584, in Lancashire or possibly the Isle of Man, and subsequently migrated to the mainland. His father, Huan Standish, apparently brought the boy up to be a fighter and encouraged him to join the army from an early age.

As something of a soldier of fortune, he followed the action. He went to Holland at the age of twenty to fight for the Dutch against the Spanish in a small force sent by Queen Elizabeth and was employed at an early age in the military service in Holland as a drummer. Although a believer in the values of the Pilgrims and a Christian, he was never a member of the Church.

Standish sailed with the original Leyden group, having been appointed military adviser and organizer of defence by Robert Cushman and John Carver. He sailed on the *Mayflower* with his wife Rose, who came from the Isle of Man. Unfortunately Rose died during the first sickness in the early winter, and Standish subsequently re-married. He died in 1656.

Standish was short, with reddish hair and a ruddy complexion, and as an experienced soldier and leader of men was apparently quite an attractive personality in the colony. Standish's matchmaking role between Priscilla Mullins and John Alden, her shy admirer, is immortalized in the Longfellow poem *The Courtship of Myles Standish*. As Captain General of the Pilgrim Fathers and a protector of the Leyden group from the start, he was always one of the staunchest supporters of the cause.

Elder William Brewster

William Brewster was the devout Moses of the tribe and the most important religious leader in the colony. For many years he served as their spiritual guide. He was a pillar of rectitude, setting high standards throughout the early years as the principal Elder in the Church.

As one of the original Pilgrims who fled to Leyden and then sailed on the *Mayflower*, Brewster provided a continuity as important as the administrative leadership of Bradford or Winslow, or the military leadership of Standish.

He was born about 1564 in Scrooby, Yorkshire, and matriculated at Cambridge University. When his father died he was promoted to the important position of Steward of the Archbishop's Manor where he managed the tavern for the King's Post riders. Brewster married a local Englishwoman, Mary, and had many children.

His intellectual abilities had been clear from the start and enabled him to gain an appointment in the diplomatic service under Sir William Davidson. Having been born to the manor and distinguished himself in this service, he was soon apprenticed in the arts of diplomacy at the courts of Elizabeth I. Following the domestic political upheavals, which culminated in the execution of Mary Queen of Scots, Brewster fell out of favor in these royal circles because of the increasing religious controversy.

He had become interested in religious affairs and, having read widely, selected the Puritan mission as his life's work. He then founded the Scrooby congregation. In order to publicize the Pilgrim cause he became a printer and publisher and distinguished himself in both England and Holland by printing brave and brutally honest religious works. He was hunted down and persecuted for printing matters of religious conviction and spent considerable periods of time in prison as a result.

Brewster was forced underground in London before the *Mayflower* sailed in order to avoid further imprisonment, and had to be smuggled onto the ship. He had established himself by 1616 as a publisher of books and pamphlets. His main inspiration was spreading religious propaganda for the Puritans and this angered King James. James ordered his arrest after the political scandals caused by the Perth Assembly; he was sentenced in 1626 for sedition to fourteen years' imprisonment, but as he was in the Colony he never had to serve out his sentence.

With Richard Clifton he organized the Separatist congregation at Scrooby and was always a 'principal member' of the Church in Leyden. He became an Elder and assistant to Reverend John Robinson, and remained an Elder until his death. He died in 1643 at the grand old age of eighty having become an archetype of the 'Pilgrim Fathers'.

John Carver

Carver was the original father figure, first Governor of the Colony and the first true leader in the new land. A foundation member of the movement he was at the Leyden congregation and was then sent to England to organize the deal for the settlement at Plymouth.

He was born in England and was baptized 9 September 1565 at Doncaster, Yorkshire, seven miles from Austerfield, next to Bentley — not far from where William Bradford was born. He was in fact one of the earliest associates of William Brewster and Bradford, and the brother-in-law of the Pilgrim's spiritual leader Reverend John Robinson. He was a well-to-do London merchant who joined the Leyden congregation about 1610. Chief organizer of the London contingent, he was the actual charterer of the *Mayflower*.

Carver was apparently a deacon of the Church but had not been a member of the Scrooby congregation, because he made his own way to Holland and Leyden by 1616. As he was reputed to be rich and possessing a good business sense, he was chosen with Robert Cushman to seek the Virginia Company and to have a patent granted.

Carver married a widow, Katherine White, who was also struck down by the sickness that cut short Carver's life in the first winter of 1621.

They consequently had no issue but brought with them a servant girl called Desire Minter, three men servants, a maid servant and a boy transported under his care.

When Carver died suddenly after a day of hard work in the field in April 1621, he was aged fifty six years and was one of the oldest Pilgrims.

John Howland

Howland was one of the most enterprising men in the colony and a success story from the start. His life was an early example of what men could do if given the opportunities in the new land of America. He sailed as a servant and aide to Governor Carver but before long he was performing so well that he was appointed Assistant Governor. He played a leading role in the administration of the colony as a good, solid man who could be trusted.

Howland was born in England about 1593-94 and from an early age he travelled with the Carver family. He was there at the start as part of the Leyden congregation so was truly one of the Pilgrim Fathers. A resourceful man, he decided to stay with the Carvers believing in the Pilgrim cause. When he was swept overboard in a storm in the mid-Atlantic he had the presence of mind to reach out and grab a trailing rope and with the help of others pulled himself back out of the sea.

Although listed as a 'servant', he was more probably an 'employee' because he signed the November *Mayflower* Compact before many others and took a leading role in the exploration and settlement and then administration of the colony. He married Elizabeth Tilley and had ten children before he died in Plymouth in 1687.

Isaac Allerton

Isaac Allerton was something of a Judas among the Pilgrim group. Unlike Howland he was an example of how power can corrupt, as on achieving authority he betrayed his fellow Pilgrims for his own ends. Initially he was a fine Pilgrim who helped build the movement and create the settlement, serving as Assistant Governor to both Carver and then Bradford. The strains of making a living in the colony and the temptations proved too much for him however and he began to put his own interests ahead of the group, eventually lying and cheating and betraying the Pilgrim cause.

Born in England in 1586 he began his professional life as a tailor in London. Later he married Mary Norris in Leyden, on 4 October 1611, and was made a 'freeman' of Leyden on 7 February 1614.

He sailed with the *Mayflower* in 1620, proving a tower of strength on the voyage. He then helped with early exploring parties, with the building of the settlement, and then with its administration doing much of the vital work for the Governors whom he assisted. He put all this administrative knowledge to good use when he was appointed the foreign affairs representative and, when in England on Pilgrim business, began his own business as a merchant engaged in extensive trading in New England.

His first wife Mary gave birth to a still-born son on board the *Mayflower* in Plymouth Harbor in March 1621. She herself died one month later. But Allerton already had other children by her, including Bartholomew, Remember and Mary. He then married a daughter of Elder William Brewster.

Emotions ran high when the Pilgrims found out he was using their business mission to England to develop his own trading organization, and he became most unpopular because he had gone against some of the basic principles they believed in. The latter part of his life was difficult as the Pilgims lost faith in him and he fell out with them. He finally moved to another district. He died in shame in New Haven in 1659.

John Billington

From the start Billington was the black sheep of the Pilgrim family. Bradford claims he came from 'the profanest family' of the lot. From the start he was a villain and, as time went on and the strains of building a new world increased, he went from bad to worse.

He came from London and was possibly 'trained to husbandry'. He married an English woman, Helen, and they had two children, John and Francis. John Billington was thirty when he and his family sailed in the *Mayflower*. Bradford claims 'they were an ill-conditioned lot and unfit for the company of the planters' and 'I know not by what friend shuffled into their Company'.

Having committed the first punishable offence in 1621 by challenging the authority of his Plymouth Plantation leaders, Billington continued to rebel until he finally murdered a fellow Pilgrim, following an argument, and was executed about September 1630.

Priscilla Mullins

The pretty Priscilla was the darling of the Pilgrim colony. The daughter of William Mullins and his second wife, Alice, she was about sixteen years of age when the *Mayflower* sailed.

She alone survived when her parents were struck down by diseases soon after arrival. An attractive catch and just the right age for breeding, she was sought after by all the single men in the group. Eventually — following an introduction by Captain Myles Standish — she married the shy Southampton cooper John Alden with whom she had eleven children before dying at Duxbury in 1650.

Priscilla was the most romantic figure in the colony and the heroine of Longfellow's poem, *The Courtship of Myles Standish*, as Myles Standish and John Alden were both involved in attracting the attention of the most sought-after bride in the colony.

Mary Chilton

Among the women in the original group, Mary Chilton appears to have been the strongest and most brave and served the colony well.

On arriving in the colony she showed no hesitation at all in clambering ashore with her famous leap onto Plymouth Rock leading the way from the boat to the shore for those Pilgrims behind her who hesitated. As this tale was passed down from generation to generation, Mary has caught the imagination of Americans.

Born in 1608 the daughter of James and Susanna Chilton, she sailed with the *Mayflower* as one of 'the first comers'. During the sickness and throughout the first terrible winter she helped to tend the sick and dying playing the role of nurse. In 1627 she married John Winslow, a brother of Governor Edward Winslow, and had ten children. She died in Boston in 1679.

Other Pilgrims

There were many people who helped the Pilgrim cause but did not actually sail to America. The most prominent was perhaps their religious leader Reverend Robinson.

Reverend John Robinson

Though he did not migrate to America, Robinson was the real saint who inspired the Pilgrims. He was the earthly connection to their God; it was the inspiration that motivated them from start to finish. He was born about 1575 in England and was a Cambridge alumni in holy orders. His religious studies then inspired him to collaborate with Brewster and they organized the Separatist Church at Scrooby, which fled to Leyden. In Leyden, Robinson was very involved in the intellectual and spiritual issues of the day giving many popular lectures and writing religious articles. He became a controversial figure, acquiring many enemies as well as friends.

He was unable travel to America with the original group and although he continued to express his desire to rejoin his flock, he died in Leyden on 1 March 1625, a venerated and much-loved leader.

The 102 Pilgrims

The Pilgrims were organized into twenty-three family or household groups travelling together under the head of the family. Each family group normally consisted of husband, wife, children, servants and attached children. The author has followed the generally accepted spelling of these names which may, in some cases, differ from the spelling given by Bradford.

The first family group

1. John Carver. The first Governor of the colony, an original Leyden congregation member, provided initial leadership but died in Plymouth April 1621.
2. Katherine Carver, his wife, who died in the colony June 1621.
3. Desire Minter, Carver's servant who returned to England to die.

4. John Howland, Carver's man servant who was rescued after falling from the *Mayflower* and became Assistant Governor; married Elizabeth Tilley and had ten children.
5. Roger Wilder, Carver's man servant who died in the spring of 1621.
6. William Latham, Carver's servant boy who spent twenty years in the colony before moving to the Bahamas where he died of starvation.
7. An unnamed maid servant attached to the Carvers who married in Plymouth but died soon after.
8. Jasper More, the Carver's servant boy, who was one of the first to die on *Mayflower* in Cape Cod Harbor December 1620.

The second family group
9. William Brewster, founder of the Scrooby Pilgrim Church, the ruling Elder who died at Duxbury, 10 April 1644, at eighty years of age.
10. Mary Brewster, his wife who died before 1627.
11. Love Brewster, son of William, had four children, died at Duxbury 1650.
12. Wrestling Brewster, son of William, died in Plymouth.
13. Richard More, Brewster's servant boy and a brother of Jasper More, married and had four children, changed name to Mann, died at Salem.
14. Master More, brother of Jasper and Richard, died at Plymouth in spring of 1621.

The third family group
15. Edward Winslow, Pilgrim leader from original Leyden congregation, Governor of the colony, foreign affairs agent, married twice, left colony, died in West Indies on a mission for Oliver Cromwell in 1655.
16. Elizabeth Winslow, his first wife, died in spring 1621.
17. George Soule, Winslow's man servant had eight children, died at Duxbury 1680.
18. Elias Story, Winslow's man servant, died in Plymouth in spring of 1621.
19. Ellen More, Winslow's servant girl, sister of Jasper and Richard More.

The fourth family group
20. William Bradford, the Governor for most of the early years and official scribe, married twice, died aged sixty eight in 1657.
21. Dorothy Bradford, his first wife, who drowned in Cape Cod Harbor 7 December 1620.

The fifth family group

22. Isaac Allerton, original Pilgrim from Leyden congregation, Assistant Governor and foreign affairs agent, married three times — with his second wife being the daughter of William Brewster — initially useful settler but later betrayed Pilgrims; died 1659 in New Haven, Connecticut.
23. Mary Allerton, his first wife, died in Plymouth, spring 1621.
24. Bartholomew, son of Allerton, who returned to England and died there.
25. Remember, daughter of Allerton, married Moses Maverick, died before 1652.
26. Mary, daughter of Allerton, married Thomas Cushman (no relation to Robert), became the last surviver of the *Mayflower* Pilgrims, dying in 1699 in Plymouth.
27. John Hooke, Allerton's servant boy, died in Plymouth, spring 1621.

The sixth family group

28. Samuel Fuller, the doctor of the colony, an original Leyden congregation member and a deacon, his wife joined him later, had three children, died 1633.
29. William Button, servant to surgeon Fuller, baptized at Austerfield 12 February 1598, the only passenger to die at sea on the *Mayflower* on 6 November 1620.

The seventh family group

30. John Crackston senior, a potentially useful man who died in Plymouth in the first spring.
31. John Crackston, son of Crackston, who got lost in the woods and died of exposure in 1628.

The eighth family group

32. Captain Myles Standish, Commanding Military Officer, had an officer's commission from Queen Elizabeth, foreign affairs agent, married twice, died in 1656.
33. Rose Standish, his first wife, who died in Plymouth in spring 1621.

The ninth family group

34. Christopher Martin, treasurer for the Pilgrims, religious sympathizer, helped organize the voyage, died in Plymouth 8 January 1621.
35. Marie Martin, his wife, died early 1621.
36. Solomon Prower, Martin's servant who died in Plymouth the first winter.
37. John Langmore, Martin's servant who died in Plymouth the first winter.

The tenth family group

38. William Mullins, died in Plymouth 21 February 1621.
39. Alice Mullins, died in Plymouth in Spring 1621.
40. Joseph Mullins, son of William, died in Plymouth in Spring 1621.
41. Priscilla Mullins, daughter of William, married John Alden, had eleven children.
42. Robert Carter, Mullins's man servant, died in Spring 1621.

The eleventh family group

43. William White, a useful settler who died in Plymouth 21 February 1621.
44. Susanna, his wife, who later married Governor Edward Winslow in the first wedding in Plymouth May 1621 and died at Marshfield in 1680.
45. Resolved White, son of William, who married and had five children, died at Salem in 1680.
    Peregrene White, son of William and the first English child born in New England on *Mayflower* in Cape Cod Harbor 1620, had two children and died in Marshfield 1704.
46. William Holbeck, man servant to William White, died in Plymouth in Spring 1621.
47. Edward Thompson, man servant to William White, was the first to die in Cape Cod Harbor on *Mayflower* 4 December 1620.

The twelfth family group

48. Steven Hopkins, a Pilgrim leader who joined from London, married, had nine children, died 1644.
49. Elizabeth, his wife, died in Plymouth sometime after 1640.
50. Giles Hopkins, son of Steven, married, had ten children, died at Yarmouth in 1690.
51. Constanta Hopkins, daughter of Steven, married, had twelve children, the most children of any Pilgrim.
52. Damaris Hopkins, daughter to Steven, married Jacob Cooke, died before 1669.
    Oceanus Hopkins, the first child born to the Pilgrims on *Mayflower* while it was crossing the Atlantic, died in Plymouth in 1621.
53. Edward Doty, Hopkins's man servant from London, married twice and had nine children, died Yarmouth 1655.
54. Edward Lister, a man servant of Hopkins, moved south to Virginia and died there.

The thirteenth family group

55. Richard Warren, came alone, wife and five daughters followed, subsequently had two more sons, died 1628.

The fourteenth family group

56. John Billington, senior, head of 'one of the profanest families amongst them', trouble maker who hanged in 1630 for murder of John Newcomen.
57. Ellen Billington, his wife later married Gregory Armstrong in 1638.
58. John, son of Billington, also a trouble maker, died before 1630.
59. Francis, son of Billington, married, had eight children, died in Yarmouth 1650.

The fifteenth family group

60. Edward Tilley, member of early exploring parties, died in spring 1621.
61. Ann Tilley, his wife, died in Spring 1621.
62. Henry Sampson, a cousin, married, had seven children, died at Duxbury 1684.
63. Humility Cooper, a cousin, returned to England and died there.
64. John Tilley, brother of Edward, a member of the early exploring parties, died in Plymouth in winter of 1621.
65. Bridget Tilley, John's wife, died in the winter of 1621.
66. Elizabeth Tilley, daughter of John, married John Howland, died Plymouth 1687.

The sixteenth family group

67. Francis Cooke, married, wife and two children followed later, died 1663.
68. John Cooke, his son, married, four children, died at Dartmouth 1694.

The seventeenth family group

69. Thomas Rogers, another useful settler who died in winter of 1621.
70. Joseph Rogers, son of Thomas, later joined by brothers and sisters, married, had six children, died at Eastham 1678.

The eighteenth family group

71. Thomas Tinker, a useful settler who died in the winter of 1621.
72. Mrs Thomas Tinker, who died in the winter of 1621.
73. Master Tinker, son, died in the winter of 1621.

The nineteenth family group

74. John Rigsdale, a useful settler, who died in the winter of 1621.
75. Alice Rigsdale, his wife, who died in the winter of 1621.

The twentieth family group

76. James Chilton, a useful settler who died on 8 December 1621 on board *Mayflower* in Cape Cod Harbor.

77. Susanna Chilton, his wife, who died in the winter of 1621.
78. Mary Chilton, daughter, jumped from boat onto Plymouth Rock leading others ashore, married John Winslow (Governor Edward Winslow's brother), had nine children, died at Boston 1679.

The twenty-first family group
79. Edward Fuller, a useful settler who died in 1621.
80. Mrs Edward Fuller, who died in 1621.
81. Samuel Fuller, son of Edward, married, died in 1683 at Barnstable.

The twenty-second family group
82. John Turner, died the Winter of 1621.
83. Master Turner, son of John, who died the first winter 1621.
84. Master Turner, a second son, who died in the first winter of 1621.

The twenty-third family group
85. Francis Eaton had the good sense to bring a large iron screw onto the *Mayflower* that was used to repair broken main beam, married three times, died in Plymouth 1633.
86. Sarah Eaton, his first wife, who died in Plymouth in the winter of 1621.
87. Samuel Eaton, arrived as a baby but survived, married and died at Middleborough 1648.

The single men
88. Moses Fletcher, died winter 1621.
89. Thomas Williams, died winter 1621.
90. John Goodman, a settler who got lost soon after landing, then died before spring 1621.
91. Edmund Margesson, died in winter 1621.
92. Richard Clarke, died winter 1621.
93. Richard Britteridge, a settler who was among the first to die on *Mayflower* at Cape Cod, 21 December 1620.
94. Digory Priest, a settler who was married to Isaac Allerton's sister, was among the first to die on New Year's Day 1621, wife and children followed later and survived.
95. Richard Gardiner, survived to become a sailor but died on an expedition overseas.
96. Gilbert Winslow, brother of Governor Winslow, who returned to England and died there.
97. Peter Browne, married twice, had two children by each wife and died in Plymouth 1633.
98. John Alden, a cooper hired at Southampton to make barrels and perform other duties and who decided to stay and join the settlement, married Priscilla Mullins in the colony's major romance, had eleven children and died at Duxbury 1687.

99. John Allerton, hired as a sailor, planned to collect second shipload and guide them to the settlement but died in first winter of 1621.
100. Thomas English, hired as the master of the long boat or shallop, died in winter 1621.
101. William Trevore, hired as a sailor, helped the Pilgrims for a year but then returned to England.
102. Mr Ellis, hired as a sailor, helped the Pilgrims for a year but then returned to England.

The Pilgrim Ship — The Mayflower

The ship which carried the Pilgrims across the seas was both an attractive ship and a good solid workhorse. It is little wonder that she has become the darling of American maritime history.

She was a three-masted, fully-rigged ship carrying square sails on every mast; but she was tiny as she only weighed 180 tons and was only ninety feet long on deck and twenty two feet wide. She had an unbelievably shallow depth of fourteen feet. Yet this ship carried 152 people on the voyage — 102 Pilgrims and about fifty crew, which alone was something of a miracle.

The *Mayflower*'s home port in 1620 was London and she sailed under the flag of the Union Jack as decreed by James I in 1606. As just an ordinary commercial trading vessel she was one of thousands; although her name was more attractive than many, conjuring up, as it did, optimistic images of the English spring. But for her work in the service of the Pilgrims, however, she would have disappeared in the historical records.

She was initially employed as a wine ship trading between England and Mediterranean ports, being then owned by Christopher Nichols, Robert Child, Thomas Short and Christopher Jones. Jones was also her captain and the one who sailed her with the first Pilgrims to New England. Captain Jones and Robert Child still owned their quarter shares in her, and it was from them that the Pilgrims chartered her in the summer of 1620 to undertake this epic voyage.

She sailed into the Pilgrim story in 1620, when she was picked from the London pool of ships to take a batch of immigrants to America. She embarked about sixty five of her passengers at London near Wapping, about the middle of July and proceeded down the Thames into the English Channel and then on to Southampton Water, where she met up with the *Speedwell*. Although the *Speedwell* proved unseaworthy, the *Mayflower* performed well and reached America safely after a voyage of nine weeks.

Her skipper was Captain Jones and the ship's Governor was Christopher Martin. She carried four mates — John Clarke (pilot), after whom Clarke Island was named in the new colony; Robert Coppin (pilot); Andrew Williamson; and John Parker. She also carried four quartermasters and a surgeon — Dr. Giles Heale — besides a carpenter, cooks, the cooper John Alden, boatswains, gunners and about thirty six men before the mast. This gave her a total complement of fifty.

The *Mayflower* remained in the colony for several months before returning to England and embarking on a series of successful commercial ventures. She then disappeared from the records.

As a ship, she was rather squat, though not unshapely, built with high poop and forecastle, broad of beam, short in the waist, confined between decks and designed for carrying cargo rather than for speed — which was a characteristic of the square rig of her time, when little use was made of the fore and aft sails.

She had four main decks — the highest at the stern called the poop deck, the main deck out in the open running from the bow to the stern and then a deck below this where the people lived, slept and ate; and finally another deck further below where the supplies were stored.

There were also cabins of different sizes. The Captain's cabin was of course the largest and most comfortable but there was also a main cabin for the Pilgrims and other more makeshift cabins built between decks to accommodate all the extra people on the voyage. Family groups had a cabin where possible; John Billington certainly enjoyed one but most of the single men and boys slept in bunks between decks.

In addition there was a galley area with a hearth box where meals could be cooked on a fire and people could huddle around and keep warm. Buckets served as toilets and had to be tipped out over the side when used.

The *Mayflower* carried guns, of course, to protect herself from pirates. In fact the second ship to bring Pilgrims to the colony, the *Fortune* was captured by pirates. There were a magazine, and carpenters' and sailmakers' lockers. There were also compasses and other navigational equipment in general use by most ships.

On board the *Mayflower* the Pilgrims also carried a boat of their own called a shallop. This open sloop of thirty feet and about ten tons had both oars and a sail. There was also a smaller boat, and the Captain had a skiff for his own use.

2 Escape From England
1606–1608

> 'Being thus constrained to leave their
> native soyle and countrie, their lands &
> livings, and all their friends & famillier
> acquaintance, it was much, and thought
> marvelous by many. But to goe into a
> countrie they knew not (but by hearsay),
> wher they must learne a new language,
> and get their livings they knew not how,
> it being a dear place, & subjecte to the
> misseries of warr, it was by many
> thought an adventure almost desperate, a
> case intolerable, & a misserie worse then
> death'
>
> William Bradford

1606 Bradford begins his story with the religious conflict and persecution in England, which drove puritan groups like his Pilgrims from their native soil. To start with he says in order to 'truly unfould, I must begine at the very roote & rise of the same. The which I shall endevor to manefest in a plaine stile, with singuler regard unto the simple trueth in all things, at least as near as my slender judgmente can attaine the same'.

Referring to the religious upheavals which had divided England since the break from the Roman Catholic church by Henry VIII who created the Church of England, Bradford tells of the dreadful persecution that had swept around the country like a wive of terror. Attacking the catholics for ushering in a new dark age he complains, 'It is well knowne unto the godly and judicious, how ever since the first breaking out of the lighte of the gospell in our Honourable Nation of England,' that there had been periods of 'grosse darknes of popery which had covered & overspred the Christian worled'.

Bradford claims that puritan groups like his Pilgrims or saints, as he called his sect, were persecuted through 'warrs & opposissions ever since, Satan hath raised, maintained, and continued against the Sainects, from time to time, in one sorte or other'.

He claims that dissenting religious groups were punished by the government and orthodox church in a cruel manner. 'Some times by

The Puritan preachers of the day who opposed the decadence of the popular church demanded a strict adherence to their doctrine and were prepared to die for their beliefs.

bloody death and cruell torments; other whiles imprisonments, banishments, & other hard usages; as being loath his kingdom should goe downe'. These were troubled times but nevertheless Bradford was optimistic claiming that eventually he would see 'the trueth prevaile, and the churches of God reverte to their anciente puritie, and recover their primative order, libertie, & bewtie'.

He feared in the meantime that conditions could become increasingly threatening in England for the puritan groups like his Pilgrims who saw themselves as 'sincere servants of God' because Roman Catholic or 'papist' forces raised their heads from time to time as the Devil Satan 'then begane to take him to his anciente strategemes, used of old against the first Christians' and 'then begane to sow errours, heresies, and wounderfull dissentions amongst the professours them selves, (working upon their pride & ambition, with other corrupte passions incidente to all mortall men, yea to the saints them selves in some measure,) by which wofull effects followed; as not only bitter contentions, & harrburnings, schismes, with other horrible confusions, but Satan tooke occasion & advantage therby to foyst in a number of vile ceremoneys, with many unproffitable cannons & decrees, which have since been as snares to many poore & peaceable souls even to this day'.

Punishment against puritan groups in England had become severe by the start of the seventeenth century, Bradford said, causing many to flee from England in the same manner that he and his fellow Pilgrims would be forced to do. He claimed the violence against purist religious groups could be terrifying and 'was no less than that of ould practised towards the Christians when they were compelled & drawne to sacrifice to idoles; for many indured sundrie kinds of tormente, often rackings, & dismembering of their joynts; confiscating of ther goods; some bereaved of their native soyle; other departed this life under the hands of the tormentor; and some died in banishmete, & never saw ther cuntrie againe' and these victims of religious persecution had to be counted against 'those worthy martires & confessors which were burned in queene Marys days & otherwise tormented, many (both students & others) fled out of the land, to the number of 800'.

Religious refugees formed new churches abroad once they escaped and 'became severall congregations' in European towns such as 'Wesell, Frankford, Bassill, Emden, Markpurge, Strausborugh, & Geneva', although, once abroad, these people inevitably became embroiled in a 'bitter warr of contention & persecution about the ceremonies, & servise-booke, and other popish and antichristian stuffe, the plague of England to this day'.

Bradford claimed that the religious conflict dividing England was now being fought between his Pilgrims who had formed a group of separatists to return to the New Testament's simplicity so they could worship God in their own manner on the one hand, and the newly-established and wealthy Church of England with its corrupt bishops

William Bradford was born in this solid country house in the English village of Austerfield.

and church hierarchy on the other hand. The Pilgrims complained that the Church surrounded itself with the trappings of temporal power and lavish pomp and ceremony, and that it claimed total jurisdiction on all forms of worship in England by laying down the rules and outlawing the Pilgrims' style of worship.

Bradford believed that his 'side laboured to have the right worship of God & discipline of Christ established in the church, according to the simplicitie of the gospell, without the mixture of mens inventions, and to have & to be ruled by the laws of Gods word, dispensed in those offices, & by those officers of Pastors, Teachers, & Elders, & according to the Scripturs'. While in direct opposition the 'other partie, though under many colours & pretences, endevored to have the episcopall dignitie (after the popish manner) with their large power & jurisdiction still retained; with all those courts, cannons, & ceremonies, togeather with all such livings, revenues, & subordinate officers, with other such means as formerly upheld their antichristian greatnes, and enabled them with lordly & tyranous power to persecute the poore servants of God'.

Bradford also feared that the Catholic revival had a tendency to reoccur from time to time; it would enter the country like an insidious fifth column and threaten the simplicity of his Pilgrim group. 'And this contetion dyed not with queene Mary, nor was left beyonds the seas, but at her death these people returning into England under gracious queene Elizabeth, many of them being preferred to bishopricks & other promotions, according to their aimes and desires, that inveterate hatered against the holy disciple of Christ in his church hath continued to this day. In somuch that for fear it should preveile, all plotts & devices have been used to keepe it out, incensing the queene & state against it as dangerous for the common wealth'.

His Pilgrim group wanted to be separate and distinct and not confused with any others, like the puritans, as a whole. But it was not easy for them; they were smeared by their opponents who in an attempt 'to cast contempte the more upon the sincere servants of God', then insulted them when they 'most injuriously gave unto & imposed upon them, that name of Puritans'. This insult which undermined his group had a profound effect as he explained: 'And lamentable it is to see the effects which have followed. Religion hath been disgraced, the godly greeved, afflicted, persecuted, and many exiled, sundrie have lost their lives in prisones & otherways. On the other hand, sin hath been countenanced, ignorance, profannes, & atheisme increased, & the papists encouraged to hope againe for a day'.

The pure Christian beliefs of his Pilgrims were increasingly attacked and the 'more it is published, the more it is contemned & reproached of many'. Ironically 'not prophanes nor wickednes, but Religion it selfe is a byword, a moking-stock, & a matter of reproach; so that in England at this day the man or woman that begines to profes Religion, & to serve

William Bradford's early religious philosophy began forming at this local church in Austerfield.

God, must resolve with him selfe to sustaine mocks & injueries even as though he lived amongst the enimies of Religion. And this comone experience hath confirmed & made too apparente'.

This general climate of repression affected Bradford and his particular Pilgrim group who lived 'in the North parts' forcing them to consider leaving the country. He explains that many had begun 'to reforme their lives, and make conscience of their wayes' but 'the worke of God was no sooner manifest in them' than 'they were both scoffed and scorned by the profane multitude, and the ministers urged with the yoak of subscription, or els must be silenced'.

As a result, Bradford's group realised that 'not only these base and beggerly ceremonies were unlawfull, but also that the lordly & tiranous power of the prelats ought not to be submitted unto'. His fellow Pilgrims knew that this persecution was 'contrary to the freedome of the gospell, would load & burden mens consciences, and by their compulsive power make a prophane mixture of persons & things in the worship of God'.

Thus they believed there was no alternative but to go their own way and follow their conscience, especially as they had seen 'the evill of these things, in thes parts, and whose harts the Lord had touched with heavenly zeale for his trueth'. So they created a daring plan of action and 'shooke off this yoake of antichristian bondage, and as the Lords free people, joyned them selves (by a convenant of the Lord) into a church estate, in the felowship of the gospell, to walke in all his wayes, made known, or to be made known unto them, according to their best endeavours, whatsoever it should cost them, the Lord assisting them. And that it cost them something this ensewing historie will declare'.

In the end the group of Pilgrims that eventually fled to America 'were of sundrie townes & vilages, some in Notinghamshire, some of Lincollinshire, and some of Yorkshire'. Initially these Pilgrims were led by a 'Mr. Richard Clifton, a grave & reverend preacher, who by his paines and dilligens had done much good, and under God had ben a means of the conversion of many. And also that famous and worthy man Mr. John Robinson, who afterwards was their pastor for many years, till the Lord tooke him away by death. Also Mr. William Brewster a reverent man, who afterwards was chosen an elder of the church and lived with them till old age'.

1607   Conditions became impossible by 1607 and the little band of Pilgrims decided to escape the terrible persecution because 'they could not long continue in any peaceable condition, but were hunted & persecuted on every side, so as their former afflictions were but as flea-bitings in comparison of these which now came upon them. For some were taken & clapt up in prison, others had their houses besett & watcht night and day, & hardly escaped their hands: and the most were faine to flie & leave their howses & habitations, and the means of their livelehood'.

*Because of their nonconformist religious opinions some of the Pilgrims
were clapped into prison in the early years of the sixteenth century,
which strengthened their resolve to flee the country.*

Ye fhalbe led before Princes
and rulers for my names fake.
Math. 10.

*Those English Puritans and Pilgrims persecuted for their religious
beliefs took heart from the biblical prophecy 'Ye shall be led before
Princes and rulers for my name's sake'.*

*The Dutch university town of Leyden became the first real home for the
Pilgrims as here they found religious freedom and employment.*

*The Pilgrims found a ship to transport them to America from among
the ships in the Delfthaven waters.*

With 101 Pilgrims, a crew of nearly 50 and supplies intended to last the new colony for a year, the little Mayflower had to be economically packed for the voyage.

The anticipation had reached such a peak by the time the day of departure arrived that the Mayflower received a rousing send-off as she weighed anchor in Plymouth Harbor.

The Mayflower *and* Speedwell *were forced to drop anchor in the mouth of Dartmouth Harbor because by then the* Speedwell *was leaking badly and in need of repair.*

After their frightening voyage, a new dawn seemed to herald the Pilgrims on their safe arrival in America.

Standish church was one of the many places of worship attended by the English puritans who had begun developing their own nonconformist philosophy.

The prison sentences were the last straw and made them turn their back on their beloved England. So they decided to flee to enlightened Holland where freedom of religion had been allowed since the second half of the sixteenth century. Explaining their decision Bradford wrote: 'seeing them selves thus molested, and that ther was no hope of their continuance ther, by a joynte consente they resolved to goe into the Low Countries, wher they heard was freedome of Religion for all men; as also how sundrie from London, & other parts of the land, had been exiled and persecuted for the same cause, & were gone thither, and lived at Amsterdam, & in other places of the land'.

Following considerable planning sessions and correspondence with authorities in Holland where there were already other break-away English churches, Bradford related: 'So affter they had continued togeither aboute a year, and kept their meetings every Saboth in one place or other, exercising the worship of God amongst them selves, not withstanding all the dilligence & malice of their adverssaries, they seeing they could no longer continue in that condition, they resolved to get over into Holland as they could; which was in the year 1607 & 1608'.

The die was cast. The first step of the Pilgrims' American journey had been taken.

Bradford explained with some feeling how the Pilgrims were forced to leave their loved ones to set out for the land where they could worship in peace but where they were to be confronted by a new set of problems. 'Being thus constrained to leave their native soyle and countrie, their lands & livings, and all their friends & famillier acquaintance, it was much, and thought marvelous by many. But to goe into a countrie they knew not (but by hearsay), wher they must learne a new language, and get their livings they knew not how, it being a dear place, & subjecte to the misseries of warr, it was by many thought an adventure almost desperate, a case intolerable, & a misserie worse then death'.

Holland was selected by the Pilgrims because in 1579 at the Union of the Provinces it was laid down that 'every citizen should remain free in his religion, and no man be molested or questioned on the subject of divine worship'. Nevertheless it was going to be a difficult transition for these simple folk: 'Espetially seeing they were not aquainted with trads nor traffique, (by which that countrie doth subsiste,) but had only been used to a plaine countrie life, and the inocente trade of husbandrey'. Not that their escape from England was by any means straightforward, either; their passage was barred by treacherous opponents on both land and sea 'for though they could not stay, yet were the not suffered to goe, but the ports & havens were shut against them, so as they were faine to seek secrete means of conveance, & to bribe & fee the mariners, & give exterordinarie rates for their passages. And yet were they often times betrayed (many of them), and both they & their goods intercepted & surprised, and therby put to great trouble & charge'.

Most of the English Pilgrims came from simple rural villages where little had changed for centuries.

People were not allowed to travel overseas without a licence in the early seventeenth century and such permits were certainly not issued to religious dissenters, so the escape route was barred from the start. To overcome this the Pilgrims arranged a transportation deal with commercial carriers. But then, as they attempted to leave England by sea in November 1607, they were betrayed by their own countrymen: 'Ther was a large companie of them purposed to get passage at Boston in Lincoln-shire, and for that end had hired a shipe wholy to them selves, & made agreement with the maister to be ready at a certaine day, and take them and their goods in, at a conveniente place, wher they accordingly would all attende in readines. So after long waiting, & large expences, though he kepte not day with them, yet he came at length & tooke them in, in the night. But when he had them & their goods abord, he betrayed them, haveing before hand complotted with the serchers & other officers so to doe; who tooke them, and put them into open boats, & ther rifled & ransaked them, searching them to their shirts for money, yea even the women furder then became modestie; and then caried them back into the towne, and made them a spectackle & wonder to the multitude, which came flocking on all sids to behould them'.

Following this frightening false start the first group of Pilgrims heading for Holland were then jailed despite their innocence, which split the group. This caused further delays for the leaders: 'after a months imprisonmente, the greatest parte were dismiste, and sent to the places from whence they came; but 7 of the principall' including William Brewster, the Congregation's religious Elder and Bradford himself 'were still kept in prison, and bound over to the Assises'.

April 1608

Having learnt their lesson, however, the determined Pilgrims tried again, this time from the Lincolnshire seaport of Grimsby near the mouth of the Humber: 'The nexte spring after, ther was another attempte made by some of these & others, to get over at an other place. And it so fell out, that they light of a Dutchman at Hull, having a ship of his owne belonging to Zealand; they made agreemente with him', and acquainted him with their condition, 'hoping to find more faithfullness in him, then in the former of their owne nation. He bad them not fear, for he would doe well enough. He was by appointment to take them in betweene Grimsbe & Hull, where was a large commone a good way distante from any towne'.

This second attempt did not prove much better, however; the men escaped to sea but the women were left behind: 'after the first boat full was gott abord, & she was ready to goe for more, the master espied a greate company, both horse & foote, with bills, & gunes, & other weapons; for the countrie was raised to take them. The Dutch-man seeing that, swore his countries oath, "sacremente", and having the wind faire, waiged his Ancor, hoysed sayles, & away. But the poore men

An Elizabethan town house in Lincolnshire's Boston, renowned for its conservatism and resistance to change.

which were gott abord, were in great distress for their wives and children, which they saw thus to be taken, and were left destitute of their helps; and them selves also, not having a cloath to shifte them with, more then they had on their baks, & some scarce a peney aboute them, all they had being abord the barke. It drew tears from their eyes, and any thing they had they would have given to have been a shore againe; but all in vaine, there was no remedy, they must thus sadly part'.

Misery was then heaped on misery. The heartbroken Pilgrims, having left their wives on dry land were then hurled into a most severe storm from which many feared they would never emerge. They 'endured a fearful storme at sea, being 14 days or more before they arived at their porte, in 7 whereof they neither saw son, moone, nor stars, & were driven near the coast of Norway; the mariners them selves often despairing of life; and once with shriks & cries gave over all, as if the ship had been foundred in the sea, & they sinking without recoverie. But when mans hope & helpe wholy failed, the Lords power & mercie appeared in ther recoverie; for the ship rose againe, & gave the mariners courage againe to manage her'.

What should have been a voyage of two days had become a two weeks' nightmare: 'water rane into their mouthes & ears; & the mariners cried out, We sinke, we sinke; they cried' but 'the ship did not only recover, but shortly after the violence of the storme begane to abate, and the Lord filed their afflicted minds with shuch comforts' and then 'in the end brought them to their desired Haven', the port of Amsterdam. At last the first group had arrived in the land of religious freedom.

Meanwhile, back on shore in England, the stranded Pilgrim group had had to run for their lives: 'The rest of the men that were in greatest danger, made shift to escape away before the troope could surprise them'. They must have been a sorry sight: 'weeping & crying on every side, some for their husbands, that were caried away in the ship' and 'others not knowing what should become of them, & their litle ones, others againe melted in teares, seeing their poore litle ones hanging aboute them, crying for feare, and quaking with could. Being thus aprehended, they were hurried from one place to another, and from one justice to another, till in the ende they knew not what to doe with them.'

Eventually, however, 'after they had been thus turmolyed a good while, and conveyed from one constable to another' Bradford said the English authorities expelled them: 'they were glad to be ridd of them in the end upon any termes; for all were wearied & tired with them'.

August 1608

By August 1608 everybody in the initial group of Pilgrims had escaped to Amsterdam where they could enjoy religious freedom. Already they had carved a name for themselves; their dramatic exit from England had made the Pilgrims famous overnight. They were now a group with

It was in the pews of such little churches as the Standish Chapel that the ideas of the English Pilgrims began to form.

a formidable reputation and this was part of 'the fruite that came hearby for by these so publick troubls, in so many eminente places, their cause became famouss, & occasioned many to looke into the same; and their godly cariage & Christian behaviour was such as left a deep impression in the minds of many'.

Thus approximately 125 Pilgrims from Nottinghamshire, Lincolnshire and Yorkshire had transferred their Church group to Amsterdam. Now began the task of finding accommodation, obtaining employment and establishing a puritan-style church in the unique faith that the Pilgrims had created as their own brand of Christianity.

It was one thing to escape from oppression but another thing to create a new model society for themselves abroad. For these simple rural folk, the task must have seemed formidable. They were setting out on an unchartered course and it was fortunate for them they had their principles to guide them.

3 Lying Low in Leyden
1608–1619

'Yet seeing them selves thus molested,
and that ther was no hope of their
continuance ther, by a joynte consente
they resolved to goe into the Low
Countries, wher they heard was
freedome of Religion for all men'.
William Bradford

September 1608

By September 1608 the last of the Pilgrim refugee group had arrived in Amsterdam. They were relieved to be out of oppressive England and at first it seemed they had come to the right place. This was after all the Golden Age of the Dutch Republic, whose power and influence was increasing, putting the country in the forefront of European nations. As Holland was the most solvent state in Europe, enjoying solid economic prosperity, religious tolerance and freedom of the press — including the right to publish religious tracts — it was initially a perfect haven for religious refugees like the Pilgrims.

Even so, the Pilgrims had problems assimilating in their new home: 'Being now come into the Low Countries, they saw many goodly & fortified cities, strongly walled and garded with troopes of armed men. Also they heard a strange & uncouth language, and beheld the differente manners & customes of the people, with their strange fashons and attires; all so farre differing from that of their plaine countrie villages (wherin they were bred, & had so longe lived) as it seemed they were come into a new world'.

Nevertheless, Bradford conjectured that it was not to be the strangeness of their new home which would be their main concern, but simply finding the means to escape poverty and starvation: 'But these were not the things they much looked on, or long tooke up their thoughts; for they had other work in hand, & an other kind of warr to wage & maintaine. For though they saw faire & bewtiful cities, flowing with abundance of all sorts of welth & riches, yet it was not longe before they saw the grimme & grisly face of povertie coming upon them like

27

an armed man, with whom they must bukle & incounter, and from whom they could not flye; but they were armed with faith & patience against him, and all his encounters; and though they were sometimes foyled, yet by Gods assistance they prevailed and got the victorie'.

The first thing the Pilgrims had to establish, of course, was their church which they had already fought so hard to preserve. Once the last of the leaders arrived, plans were laid for organizing a religious institution along the lines which best suited the Pilgrims. 'Now when Mr. Robinson, Mr. Brewster, & other principall members were come over, (for they were of the last, & stayed to help the weakest over before them) such things were thought on as were necessarie for their setling and best ordering of the church affairs'.

February 1609 Despite its comparative advantages, by the beginning of 1609 the Pilgrims had become disenchanted with Amsterdam as a home for their church so they applied to the Burgomasters of the University town of Leyden, thirty eight miles south of Amsterdam, for permission to settle in the more intellectually stimulating climate of that city. Leyden boasted a university which, although only founded in 1575, claimed to be in the forefront of scholarship in Christendom, employing the leading scholars such as Scaliger, Heinsius, Arminius, Vorstius, Golius and Cluvier.

The Pilgrims were granted permission to move to Leyden on 12 February and then transferred their church not long after. As Bradford explained: 'when they have lived at Amsterdam aboute a year, Mr. Robinson, their pastor, and some others of best discerning', then 'thought it was best to remove' to Leyden which offered a much more spiritual environment than that of the heavily commercialized trading port of Amsterdam, even though they would lose out financially. They 'well knew it would be much to the prejudice of their outward estats, both at presente & in licklyhood in the future; as indeed it proved to be'.

Once they had reached Leyden, the Pilgrims were happy to a man as this was 'a fair & bewtifull citie, and of a sweete situation, but made more famous by the universitie wherwith it is adorned, in which of late had been so many learned men'. At the same time however he acknow-ledged the commercial price they had paid and the fact that they would have to work hard to make ends meet. 'But wanting that traffike by sea which Amsterdam injoyes, it was not so beneficiall for their outward means of living & estats. But being now hear pitchet they fell to such trads & imployments as they best could; valewing peace & their spiri-tuall comforte above any other riches whatsoever. And at lenght they came to raise a competente & comforteable living, but with hard and continuall labor'.

In Leyden the Pilgrims church was at last united and able to grow. Before long, under the leadership of the Reverend John Robinson, it

With the freedom of religion in Leyden the Pilgrims were able to worship in such churches as St. Peter's.

became one of the leading Christian groups in the region. The congregation was free of factionalism, while Robinson himself gained a reputation for his relatively broad views and human sympathy. They obtained work and earned their daily bread in a variety of occupations: Bradford worked with a silk manufacturer; Brewster worked as a printer; and others, who had taken their own looms with them, were employed as weavers.

Bradford attributed their success to Robinson and Brewster: 'Being thus setled (after many difficulties) they continued many years in a comfortable condition, injoying much sweete & delightefull societie & spirituall comforte togeather in the wayes of God, under the able ministrie, and prudente governmente of Mr. John Robinson, & Mr. William Brewster, who was an assistante unto him in the place of an Elder, unto which he was now called & chosen by the church. So as they grew in knowledge & other gifts & graces of the spirite of God, & lived togeather in peace, & love, and holines; and many came unto them from diverse parts of England, so as they grew a great congregation'.

Throughout the next decade the congregation grew until there were 'about three hundred communicants', with the number of converts increasing annually from the Protestant French-speaking Walloons and other refugee groups. As with any puritanical group there were of course ideological conflicts with which from time to time they had to deal: 'the church purged of those that were incurable & incorrigible, when, after much partience used, no other means would serve, which seldom came to pass'. That this did not have to happen was due to the brilliant leadership of Robinson, Bradford claims: 'such was the mutuall love, & reciprocall respecte that this worthy man had to his flocke, and his flocke to him', and in fact 'it was hard to judge wheather he delighted more in haveing shuch a people, or they in haveing such a pastor'.

Even at this stage the Pilgrim church demanded a high level of community commitment; Robinson was angered by the more selfish members of the congregation: 'And none did more offend him then those that were close and cleaving to them selves, and retired from the commone good'.

During their time in Leyden the Pilgrims lived in the south-western part of the city near St. Peter's Church (Pieterskerk), congregating in the large open marketplace where they bought their food supplies and discussed the religious and political issues of the day. Robinson, of course, spent much of his time at the University of Leyden where the popularity of his lectures kept him in constant demand. The printer and religious Elder William Brewster lived in Smelly Alley (Stincksteeg).

1611 Two years after arriving in Leyden, the Pilgrims bought a large house in Bell Alley (Klooksteeg), off St. Peter's Square, to use as a headquarters for meetings of the congregation. This meeting house, called the Green

Life was peaceful for the Pilgrims in Leyden and for some years they managed to assimilate, taking their place in the local community.

Gate (Groenepoort), was also used as a parsonage; Robinson lived there with his wife Bridget, three children and a maid.

By now the Pilgrims had become very popular in Leyden. Bradford claimed this was because they were honest and hardworking. Consequently 'though many of them weer poore, yet ther was none so poore, but if they were known to be of that congregation' the Dutch, whether they were bakers or members of some other profession, 'would trust them in any reasonable matter when they wanted money. Because they had found by experience how carfull they were to keep their word, and saw them so painfull & dilligente in their callings; yea, they would strive to gett their custome, and to imploy them above others, in their worke, for their honestie & diligence'.

Through their outstanding leader Reverend Robinson, the Pilgrims had even distinguished themselves by delivering lectures in support of a number of worthwhile religious causes at a time when, 'ther were dayly & hote disputs in the schooles ther aboute' and 'the cheefe preachers of the citie, desired Mr. Robinson to dispute against' them 'but he was loath, being a stranger; yet the other did importune him, and tould him that such was the abilitie and nimblnes of the adversarie, that that truth would suffer if he did not help them. So as he condescended, & prepared him selfe against the time; and when the day came, the Lord did so help him to defend the truth & foyle this adversarie, as he put him to an apparent nonplus, in this great & publike audience. And the like he did a 2 or 3 time, upon such like occasions. The which as it caused many to praise God that the trueth had so famous victory, so it procured him much honour & respecte from those lerned men & others which loved the trueth'.

1617 During the many years they were in Leyden, the social and political climate changed, forcing the Pilgrims to think about moving to another country. The peace that they had enjoyed in Holland was now no longer guaranteed, because the treaty with the militant Spanish was about to expire and soldiers in the service of the Spanish Inquisition could then enter Holland at any moment. 'After they had lived in this citie about some 11 or 12 years, (which is the more observable being the whole time of that famose truce between that state & the Spaniards,) and sundrie of them were taken away by death, & many others begane to be well striken in years, the grave mistris Experience haveing taught them many things, those prudent governours with sundrie of the sagest members begane both deeply to apprehend their present dangers, & wisely to foresee the future, & thinke of timly remedy'.

According to Bradford the Pilgrims decided to leave Leyden 'Not out of any newfanglednes, or other such like giddie humor, by which men are oftentimes transported to their great hurt & danger, but for sundrie weightie & solid reasons' including 'the hardnes of the place & countrie' which was so difficult to endure that 'few in comparison would come to them, and fewer that would bide it out, and continew with them'. Even inspired Pilgrims 'could not endure that great labor and hard fare, with other inconveniences which they underwent & were contented with'.

Some of the Pilgrims were also growing too old for such an arduous life: 'old age began to steale on many of them, (and their great & continuall labours, with other crosses and sorrows, hastened it before the time) so as it was not only probably thought, but apparently seen, that within a few years more they would be in danger to scatter, by necessities pressing them, or sinke under their burdens, or both'.

In addition, the Pilgrims feared that the hard life in Holland was distracting their children away from the straight and narrow path of the Pilgrim way: 'many of their children, that were of best dispositions and gracious inclinations, haveing lernde to bear the yoake in their youth, and willing to bear parte of their parents burden, were, often times, so oppressed with their hevie labours, that though their minds were free and willing, yet their bodies bowed under the weight of the same, and became decreped in their early youth; the vigor of nature being consumed in the very budd as it were. But that which was more lamentable, and of all sorowes most heavie to be borne, was that many of their children, by these occasions, and the great licentiousnes of youth in that countrie, and the manifold temptations of the place, were drawne away by evill examples into extravagante & dangerous courses, getting the raines off their neks, & departing from their parents. Some became souldiers, others tooke upon them to farr viages by sea, and other some worse courses, tending to dissolutnes & the danger of their soules, to the great greefe of their parents and dishonour of God. So that they saw their posteritie would be in danger to degenerate & be corrupted'.

Most of the Pilgrims wanted to be missionaries and spread the word of God abroad, as 'a great hope & inward zeall they had of laying some good foundation, or at least to make some way therunto, for the propagating & advancing the gospell of the kingdom of Christ in those remote parts of the world'.

The question the Pilgrims had to answer was where they should go next. They could not go back to England. There were not many sympathetic countries in Europe, itself on the brink of the Thirty Years War (1618–1648) and they were terrified that the Spanish troops would invade Holland before they could escape.

Their selection of a new home soon became a choice between America and Guiana. Initially, 'the place they had thoughts on was some of those vast & unpeopled countries of America, which are frutfull & fitt for habitation, being devoyd of all civill inhabitants, wher ther are only salvage & brutish men, which range up and downe, litle otherwise then the wild beasts of the same'.

Although some of the Pilgrim leaders advocated transferring the church to America, a large number were terrified by the inherent dangers of such a move. They cited the 'many unconceivable perills & dangers: as, besides the casulties of the seas (which none can be freed from) the length of the vioage was such, as the weake bodys of women and other persons worne out with age & traville (as many of them were) could never be able to endure. And yet if they should, the miseries of the land which they should be exposed unto, would be to hard to be borne; and lickly, some or all of them togeither, to consume & utterly to ruinate them'.

These Pilgrims believed that many perils awaited them in America: 'For ther they should be liable to famine, and nakednes, & the wante, in a maner, of all things. The chang of aire, diate, & drinking of water, would infecte their bodies with sore sickneses, and greevous diseases. And also those which should escape or overcome these difficulties, should yett be in continuall danger of the salvage people, who are cruell, barbarous, & most trecherous, being most furious in their rage, and merciles wher they overcome; not being contente only to kill, & take away life, but delight to tormente men in the most bloodie manner that may be; fleaing some alive with the shells of fishes, cutting of the members & joynts of others by peesmeale, and broiling on the coles, eate the collops of their flesh in their sight whilst they live; with other cruelties horrible to be related'.

The more faint-hearted of the Pilgrims were apparently put off by the discussion; Bradford reported that 'the very hearing of these things could not but move the very bowels of men to grate within them, and make the weake to quake & tremble. It was furder objected, that it would require greater summes of money to furnish such a voiage, and to fitt them with necessaries, then their consumed estats would amounte too'.

But the leaders attempted to inspire the group: 'all great & honour-able actions are accompanied with great difficulties, and must be both enterprised and overcome with answerable courages. It was granted the dangers were great, but not desperate; the difficulties were many, but not invincible. For though their were many of them likly, yet they were not cartaine; it might be sundrie of the things feared might never befale; others by providents care & the use of good means, might in a great measure be prevented'. Bradford felt that the Pilgrims were men of heart and would have a better chance to succeed than most, especially as 'their condition was not ordinarie; their ends were good & honourable; their calling lawfull, & urgente; and therfore they might expecte the blessing of God in their proceding'. And any sacrifice would be worthwhile, as 'though they should loose their lives in this action, yet might they have comforte in the same, and their endeavors would be honourable'.

Furthermore, they argued that conditions in Holland could become far worse than America: 'as great miseries might possibly befale them

Holland provided a necessary haven for the Pilgrims but the social change forced thoughts of yet another move.

in this place, for the 12 years of truce were now out, & ther was nothing but beating of drumes, and preparing for warr, the events wherof are allway uncertaine. The Spaniard might prove as cruell as the salvages of America, and the famine and pestelence as sore hear as ther, & their libertie less to looke out for remedie'.

As a result of the persuasive powers of the leaders, the Pilgrim group voted to leave Holland for the New World. 'After many other perticuler things answered & aledged on both sids, it was fully concluded by the major parte, to put this designe in execution, and to prosecute it by the best means they could'. Yet they still could not agree on a destination. America had been proposed as the first choice but not everybody accepted this selection. Once again 'they consulted what perticuler place to pitch upon, & prepare for'.

The main alternative to America was Guiana. Sir Walter Ralegh's book *Discovery of Guiana* had been published in 1596 extolling the virtues of an equatorial paradise. Ralegh wrote 'I never saw a more beautiful country, nor more lively prospects' and claimed the newly-found land was all extensive plains with lush grass on which tame deer fed by the riversides as if 'used to a keeper's call', birds 'singing on every tree with a thousand several tunes' and 'every stone that we stopped to take up promised either gold or silver'. A contemporary poem by George Chapman embellished this image even further

> *Guiana, whose rich feet are mines of gold,*
> *Whose forehead knocks against the roof of stars,*
> *Stands on her tiptoe at fair England looking,*
> *Kissing her hand, bowing her mighty breast,*
> *And every sign of all submission making*
> *To be the sister and the daughter both,*
> *Of our most sacred maid*

As a result of Guiana's sparkling reputation, many of the Pilgrims wanted to go and live in this new garden of Eden and 'had thoughts & were ernest for Guiana, or some of those fertill places in those hott climats'. Bradford continued: 'those for Guiana aledged that the cuntrie was rich, fruitfull, & blessed with a perpetuall spring, and a florishing greenes; where vigorous nature brought forth all things in abundance & plentie without any great labour or art of man'.

After Holland, where they had been forced to work hard to earn their daily bread, this life of ease would have been welcome 'as it must needs make the inhabitants rich, seing less provisions of clothing and other things would serve, than in more coulder & less frutfull countries'. Another good reason for going to Guiana was its distance from the dreaded Spanish, as 'the Spaniards (having much more then they could possess) had not yet planted there, nor any where very near the same'.

However Bradford argued that, being Pilgrims, it was not right for them to just search for an easy life; they were embarked on a far greater mission than just the search for a modern garden of Eden. The very luxuries that attracted them to Guiana could have proved their undoing. Finally, the pro-Guiana group was outvoted by the pro-America group who argued that although 'the countrie was both frutfull and pleasante, and might yeeld riches & maintenance to the possessors, more easily then the other; yet, other things considered, it would not be so fitt for them' and 'such hott countries are subject to greevuos diseases, and many noysome impediments, which other more temperate places are freer from, and would not so well agree with our English bodys. Againe, if they should ther live, & doe well, the jealous Spaniard would never suffer them long, but would displante or overthrow them, as he did the French in Florida' (where Spanish soldiers had massacred a Huguenots refugee group earlier).

The pro-Guiana group also had plenty of arguments against America, claiming that 'if they lived among the English which were ther planted, or so near them as to be under their government, they should be in as great danger to be troubled and persecuted for the cause of religion, as if they lived in England, and it might be worse. And if they lived too farr of, they should neither have succour, nor defence from them'.

Nevertheless, the choice was made 'to live as a distincte body by them selves, under the generall Government of Virginia'. After all, one of the reasons why they were leaving Holland was their fear of losing their English identity; in the English colony in America they could at least give their children the English language education they wanted for them and teach them to observe the Sabbath, unlike the Dutch whom the Pilgrim Edward Winslow claimed profaned this holy day.

The Pilgrims selected Virginia and not New England. Virginia was first settled in 1607 at Jamestown by English settlers under the authority of the Virginia Company established in 1606. Although these Virginian settlers may have been Christian, they were motivated primarily by commercial gain.

The Pilgrims certainly knew about New England. Captain John Smith's 1616 book *Description of New England* provided ample information about this area and was based on his 1614 voyage. His accounts were not as attractive as the reports from Virginia; also the Pilgrims would have been put off by the abortive 1607 Kennebec River settlement by the Plymouth Company under Sir John Popham. None of the Pilgrims wanted to start off completely on their own, so none of them put the case for New England.

Having agreed on America the Pilgrims now decided to ask the Virginia Company if it would allow them to set up a religious colony near the 1607 Jamestown settlement and the King of England if he 'would be pleased to grant them freedome of Religion' even though he had forbidden them to practise their puritan style of worship in his own kingdom. It was a bold and daring request.

August 1617	So the Pilgrims sat down in their Leyden headquarters and hatched out a plan to send two of their leaders to London — Robert Cushman, a man of the business world, and the wealthy merchant John Carver. Bradford: 'Whereupon 2 were chosen & sent in to England (at the charge of the rest) to sollicite this matter'. Fortunately their mission seemed a success, as they 'found the Virginia Company very desirous to have them goe thither, and willing to grante them a patent, with as ample priviliges as they had, or could grant to any, and to give them the best furderance they could. And some of the cheefe of that company douted not to obtaine their suite of the king for liberty in Religion, and to have it confirmed under the kings broad seale, according to their desires'.

Initially the mission seemed successful. So far the Pilgrims had obtained verbal assurances from the Virginia Company (which owned a 100 mile strip along the Atlantic coast from the 34th to 45th degree of North latitude) that they could go and settle in America.

Bradford related however that the royal permissions the Pilgrims needed 'prooved a harder peece of worke then they tooke it for'. The King was still ordering puritans and religious dissenters to conform or leave the country and was not in the mood for setting up religious havens abroad. He did however at least agree that once they were in America 'that he would connive at them, & not molest them, provided they carried them selves peacably'.

The King was not opposed to their settling America and on being told that the Pilgrims would support themselves by fishing was reported to have said, 'So, God have my soul, 'tis an honest trade. 'Twas the Apostles own calling'. But to allow or tolerate them 'by his publick authoritie, under his seale, they found it would not be'.

So unable to achieve the guarantees they wanted 'the messengers returned, and signified what diligence had bene used, and to what issue things were come'.

November 1617	Having failed in their initial attempt to gain royal sanction, the Pilgrims concentrated on concluding the deal with the Virginia Company and obtaining equipment and provisions for the voyage; so 'other messengers were dispatched, to end with the Virginia Company as well as they could. And to procure a patent with as good and ample conditions as they might by any good means obtaine. As also to treate and conclude with such merchants and other friends as had manifested their forwardnes to provoke too and adventure in this vioage'.

15 December 1617	After Cushman and Carver returned, the Pilgrims strengthened their cause by publishing a five-point statement written by Brewster and Robinson. This spelt out their position for potential investors: 1. We veryly beleeve & trust the Lord is with us, unto whom & whose service we have given our selves in many trialls; and that he will

graciously prosper our indeavours according to the simplicitie of our harts therin.

2. We are well weaned from the delicate milke of our mother countrie, and enured to the difficulties of a strange and hard land, which yet in a great parte we have by patience overcome.

3. The people are for the body of them, industrious, & frugall, we thinke we may safly say, as any company of people in the world.

4. We are knite togeather as a body in a most stricte & sacred bond and covenante of the Lord, of the violation whereof we make great conscience, and by vertue wherof we doe hould our selves straitly tied to all care of each others good, and of the whole by every one and so mutually.

5. It is not with us as with other men, whom small things can discourage, or small discontentments cause to wish them selves at home againe. We knowe our entertainmente in England, and in Holand'.

By issuing this forthright statement, the Pilgrims believed they would convince potential Virginia Company investors of their strength of purpose. They also hoped to overcome ill-founded criticisms: 'and though it be greevious unto us that such unjust insinuations are made against us, yet we are most glad of the occasion of making our just purgation unto so honourable personages'.

Eager to leave Holland and set out for America they continued to search for the necessary investors to fund the voyage and to plead with the all-powerful Virginia Company to help them with their attempts to gain the necessary permissions: 'praing that you would please with the convenientest speed that may be, to give us knowledge of thee success of the bussines with his majesties Privie Counsell'.

27 January 1618 The Pilgrims remained desperate to obtain royal assent and the backing of the Virginia Company. As a demonstration of their loyalty to the English Crown they vowed they were prepared to sacrifice their principles by acknowledging that the King was head of Church and State: 'The oath of Supremacie we shall willingly take if it be required of us, and that conveniente satisfaction be not given by our taking the oath of Alleagence'.

But even with this offer they got nowhere. Month after month dragged past with no replies to their letters; their London representatives were unable to obtain any response from the Virginia Company. They were told that these delays were caused by internal conflict within the Virginia Company itself which had split into opposing factions. Bradford: 'These things being long in agitation, & messengers passing too and againe aboute them, after all their hopes they were long delayed by many rubs that fell in the way; for at the returne of these messengers into England they found things farr otherwise then they expected. For the Virginia Counsell was now so disturbed with factions and quarrels amongst them selves, as no business could well goe forward'.

8 May 1619

Despite their anxiety to leave Holland the Pilgrims were delayed for more than a year by these continuing commercial squabbles. Their negotiator Cushman confirmed this when he wrote, 'The maine hinderance of our proceedings in the Virginia bussines, is the dissentions and factions, as they terme it, amongst the Counsell & Company of Virginia; which are such, as that ever since we came up no business could by the be dispatched'.

Indeed Cushman was the bearer of further bad tidings. He wrote that he had received word that an earlier religious mission from Holland to Virginia, under the command of a former Elder of their Church at Amsterdam, Francis Blackwell, had ended in disaster when their ship was blown off course.

Blackwell's ship had left for Virginia in the fall of 1618, overloaded with a group of religious refugees. Cushman wrote that due to rough seas and bad conditions the 'shipe came not ther till March, but going towards winter, they had still norwest winds, which carried them to the southward beyond their course. And the master of the ship & some 6 of the mariners dieing, it seemed they could not find the bay, till after long seeking & beating aboute'.

Dockside arguments between the Pilgrims and the English commercial entrepreneurs underwriting the voyage delayed the departure and threatened to undermine the expedition.

Things went from bad to worse. Captain Maggner could not find the right harbor, and Blackwell died along with the Captain and 130 others. With the cold and stormy conditions, shortage of food and water and cramped conditions, disease broke out and 'ther are dead, he saith, 130 persons, one & other in that ship; it is said there was in all an 180 persons in the ship, so as they were packed togeather like herings. They had amongst them the fluxe, and allso wante of fresh water; so as it is hear rather wondred at that so many are alive, then that so many are dead. The marchants hear say it was Mr. Blackwells faulte to pack so many in the ship; yea, & ther were great mutterings & repinings amongst them, and upbraiding of Mr. Blackwell'.

The sympathy of Bradford and the Pilgrims was tempered however because Blackwell had broken faith with them, and although 'an elder of the church at Amsterdam, a man well known of most of them. He declined from the trueth'. It was this which 'brought so great dishonour to God, scandall to the trueth, & outward ruine to them selves in this world'. Even prior to this, in England, Blackwell had acted dishonorably by denying his involvement in the Pilgrim cause and accusing another man in his stead; Blackwell 'very unworthily betrayed and accused another godly man who had escaped, that so he might slip his own neck out of the collar, & to obtaine his owne freedome brought others into bonds'.

The lesson of the ill-fated ship was not lost on the Pilgrims. Indeed, it was considered 'of instruction & good use'.

9 June, 1619

The persistence of the Pilgrims eventually paid off. At last 'after all these things, and their long attendance, they had a patent granted them, and confirmed under the Companies seale'. They had permission from the owners of the New World to go and live there and this confirmed the choice of America over Guiana once and for all. America it was.

In this patent they had to accept 'propossitions between them & such marchants & freinds as should either goe or adventure with them, and espetially' a certain Mr. Thomas Weston 'on whom they did cheefly depend for shipping and means, whose proffers had been large'. The Pilgrims were happy about these details, not knowing too much about Weston. Having accepted these requirements in principles the Pilgrims 'were requested to fitt and prepare them selves with all speed'.

The moment had come to chose who was to go to America and who was to stay in Holland. Bradford reported: 'After which they concluded both what number and what persons should prepare them selves to goe with the first; for all that were willing to have gone could not gett ready for their other affairs in so shorte a time'.

There were approximately 300 Pilgrims to choose from now. Those who were selected to go were to be led by Elder William Brewster, while the group remaining would continue to be led by Reverend John Robinson.

Given the risks of the expedition as evidenced by Blackwell's disaster, the two church groups would be associated but independent: 'It was also agreed on by mutuall consente and covenante, that those that went should be an absolute church of them selves, as well as those that staid; seing in such a dangrous vioage, and a removall to such a distance, it might come to pass they should (for the body of them) never meete againe in this world'.

Robinson's group was by no means disadvantaged by staying at home as 'It was allso promised to those that wente first, by the body of the rest, that if the Lord gave them life, & means, & opportunitie, they would come to them as soone as they could'.

Next came the task of getting transport from Holland to England where their commercial sponsors awaited them. They began 'making inquirey about the hiring & buying of shipping for their vioage' and 'some Dutchmen made them faire offers about goeing with them'.

But then their new organizer stepped in to take control of the operation: 'Thomas Weston, a merchant of London, came to Leyden about the same time, (who was well aquainted with some of them, and a furtherer of them in their former proseedings)' and he 'perswaded them to goe on (as it seems) & not to medle with the Dutch, or too much to depend on the Virginia Company; for if that failed, if they came to resolution, he and such marchants as were his freinds (together with their owne means) would sett them forth; and they should make ready, and neither feare wante of shipping nor money; for what they wanted should be provided'.

Weston convinced the eager Pilgrims to do what he wanted them to do: 'Upon which (after the formere conclusion) articles were drawne & agreed unto, and were showne unto him, and approved by him; and afterwards by their messenger (Mr. John Carver) sent into England,

As Virginia had been settled in 1607, maps and reports on this new colony had been published well before the Pilgrims sailed.

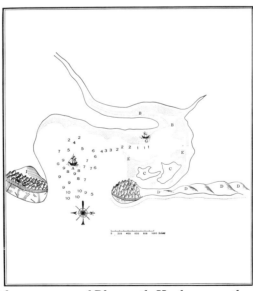

The first known map of Plymouth Harbor was the navigator Champlain's rather rudimentary sketch drawn in 1605 which recorded the depth in fathoms.

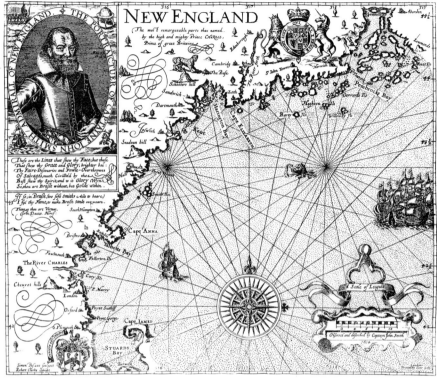

The best contemporary maps of New England were published by the legendary English explorer Captain John Smith whose 1614 chart featured most features along the coastline.

In time new settlements were started from the Colony of New Plymouth until there were Europeans all along the coast from Cape Cod Bay to Massachusetts Bay.

Although they went down on their knees to give thanks for their safe arrival the Pilgrims were presented with grave problems, as this snowswept and desolate scene depicts.

Because of the difficult conditions it was many weeks before the Pilgrims could disembark from the Mayflower and begin building their new homes.

Pilgrims and early settlers were impressed with the domestic organization within each Indian tribal group and faithfully recorded their food gathering and preparations, even if in a romanticized way.

The Pilgrims were saved from starvation when the Indian Squanto showed the new arrivals how the original Americans planted their corn in order to obtain a successful harvest.

who, togeather with Robart Cushman, were to receive the moneys & make provissione both for shiping & other things for the vioage'.

With the business arrangements out of the way and the transport organized, the time had come for the first group of Pilgrims to set out 'so those that weare to goe, prepared them selves with all speed, and sould of their estats and (such as were able) put in their moneys into the commone stock, which was disposed by those appointed, for the making of generall provissions'.

Then, just as they were leaving, they received another setback. They heard that they were to have neighbors in America to the north and they may be forced to go and live in that region instead of Virginia: 'Aboute this time also they had heard, both by Mr. Weston and others, that sundrie Honorable Lords had obtained a large grant from the king, for the more northerly parts of that countrie, derived out of the Virginia patente, and wholy secluded from their Govermente, and to be called by another name, viz. New-England. Unto which Mr. Weston, and the cheefe of them, begane to incline it was best for them to goe, as for other reasons, so cheefly for the hope of present profite to be made by the fishing that was found in that countrie'.

At this point Bradford says the setbacks and delays proved too much for the more faint-hearted Pilgrims: 'Some of those that should have gone in England, fell of & would not goe; other marchants & freinds that had offered to adventure their moneys withdrew, and pretended many excuses. Some disliking they wente not to Guiana; others againe would adventure nothing excepte they wente to Virginia. Some againe (and those that were most relied on) fell in utter dislike with Virginia, and would doe nothing if they wente thither'. For a moment it appeared as if the whole Pilgrim mission would fall apart at the seams.

As some of the more committed Pilgrims had already sold their homes and furniture, they felt betrayed: 'they of Leyden, who had put of their estats, and laid out their moneys, were brought into a greate streight, fearing what issue these things would come too'. Then to make matters worse the Pilgrim group began quarrelling over terms and conditions of their expedition. 'Mr. Weston and some others' wanted 'some of those conditions altered that were first agreed on at Leyden'. This bickering over details of their agreement continued right up to their departure.

10 June 1620 Bradford said the new terms and conditions proposed by the commercial operators backing the expedition were unacceptable to the Pilgrims who said 'our desires are that you will not entangle your selvs and us to be put in any such unreasonable courses'. The Pilgrims thought it was unfair for the investors to own so much of their property and to expect them to work every day of the week to pay back the loan and 'that the marchants should have the halfe of mens houses and lands at the dividente; and that persons should be deprived of the 2 days in a weeke agreed upon, yea every momente of time for their

The Mayflower *was just one of many commercial ships plying the waters of Europe in search of lucrative trade.*

owne perticuler; by reason wherof we cannot conceive why any should carie servants for their own help and comfort'.

Carver wrote to Cushman who was representing the Pilgrims in London, criticizing him and demanding that he create a better contract for them with the investors. But Cushman wrote back saying he was sick of receiving such 'complaints', and asked those back in Leyden 'what it is you would have of me I know not; for your crieing out, Negligence, negligence, negligence, I marvell why so negligente a man was used in the business'.

The Pilgrim group was itself starting to break up into factions. Unless they could get underway soon their whole movement was in danger of losing impetus and direction. As Cushman complained, it now seemed 'we are redier to goe to dispute, then to sett forwarde a voiage'.

Even so, the fact was that they still lacked the money to pay for the ship and goods and services needed for the 150 Pilgrims leaving initially on the expedition. Cushman explained 'We have reckoned, it should seeme, without out host; and, counting upon a 150 persons, ther cannot be found above £1200 & odd moneys of all the venturs you can reckone, besids some cloath, stockings, & shoes, which are not counted; so we shall come shorte at least 3 or £400'.

If they could not find the money then they were bound to be embarrassed by the shortfall, Cushman claimed: 'To be short, if ther be not some other dispossition setled unto them yet is, we that should be partners of humilitie and peace, shall be examples of jangling & insulting'.

11 June 1620 Despite these problems, Cushman continued negotiations with Weston, and together they hired a sixty-ton ship called the *Speedwell* which, although small, they considered would be sufficient: 'And so advising togeather we resolved to hire a ship, and have tooke liking of one till Monday, about 60 laste, for a greater we cannot gett, excepte it be tow great; but a fine ship it is. And seeing our neer freinds ther are so streite lased, we hope to assure her without troubling them any further; and if the ship fale too small, it fitteth well that such as stumble at strawes allready, may rest them ther a while'.

They were almost ready to go. Cushman requested from the group in Leyden 'that salt and netts may ther be boughte, and for all the rest we will here provid it'. Captain Reynolds was to bring the *Speedwell* from Leyden to Southampton, and additional provision had been made for the second leg from Southampton to America: 'We have hired another pilote here, one Mr. Clarke, who went last year to Virginia with a ship of kine'.

The Pilgrims had no great expectations of a New World full of riches, 'our riches shall not be in pompe, but in strenght; if God send us riches, we will imploye them to provid more men, ships, munition, &c. You may see it amongst the best pollitiks, that a commonwele is readier to ebe then to flow, when once fine houses and gay cloaths come up'.

Some of the Pilgrims were angered by the amount of money which the investors demanded from the first financial returns of the intended settlement at Plymouth and argued that the new world they were building was one of equality being created for the community not the selfish individual. 'All men are not of one condition' and 'he that is not contente his neighbour shall have as good a house, fare, means, &c. as him selfe, is not of a good qualitie'. The Pilgrims did not want selfish people either: 'Such retired persons, as have an eie only to them selves, are fitter to come wher catching is, then closing; and are fitter to live alone, then in any societie, either civill or religious'.

They agitated for a better deal than the investors in the contract. 'Our hazard is greater then theirs'. Although they do not 'urge or egg us on' as 'the motion & resolution has been always in our selves' the Pilgrims still hoped for 'equall termes & conditions' claiming that they were 'men of discretion & conscience, and so fitte to be trusted our selves with that'.

In this last minute soul-searching those few doubting Pilgrims were disappointed with those who parted ways with them in Holland: 'As for them of Amsterdam I had thought they would as soone have gone to Rome as with us; for our libertie is to them as ratts bane, and their riggour as bad to us as the Spanish Inquision.'

14 June 1620   Time continued to pass but still the ship had not sailed for England. Robinson became angry with Weston complaining about 'the estate of things hear, which indeed is very pitifull; espetialy by wante of shiping'. The delays caused by Weston and others was now considered a scandal 'But that he should not but have had either shipping ready before this time, or at least certaine means, and course, and the same known to us for it, or have taken other order otherwise, cannot in my conscience be excused'.

1 July 1620   At last the Pilgrims finalized their contract with the investors, based on their assumed future activities predicting 'that the greatest part of the Collonie is like to be imployed constantly, not upon dressing ther perticuler land & building houses, but upon fishing, trading'. This document was the basis of the relationship between the English investors (who they referred to as adventurers) and the Pilgrims (who were referred to as the planters).

The final contract was very much a commercial document demanding that the Pilgrims pay a high price for their New World.

The Pilgrim Contract   1. The adventurers & planters doe agree, that every person that goeth being aged 16. years & upward, be rated at £10, and ten pounds to be accounted a single share.

2. That he that goeth in person, and furnisheth him self out with £10. either in money or other provissions, be accounted as haveing £20 in stock, and in the devission shall receive a double share.

The smaller Speedwell *was chosen from among hundreds of similar ships in London*

3. The persons transported & the adventurers shall continue their joynt stock & partnership togeather, the space of 7 years, excepte some unexpected impedimente doe cause the whole company to agree otherwise, during which time all profits & benefits that are gott by trade, traffick, trucking, working, fishing, or any other means of any person or persons, remaine still in the commone stock untill the division.

4. That at their comming ther, they chose out such a number of fitt persons, as may furnish their ships and boats for fishing upon the sea; imploying the rest in their severall faculties upon the land; as building houses, tilling, and planting the ground, & makeing shuch commodities as shall be most usefull for the collonie.

5. That at the end of the 7 years, the capitall & profits, viz. the houses, lands, goods and chatles, be equally devided betwixte the adventurers, and planters; which done, every man shall be free from other of them of any debt or detrimente concerning this adventure.

6. Whosoever cometh to the colonie herafter, or putteth any into the stock, shall at the end of the 7 years be allowed proportionably to the time of his so doing.

7. He that shall carie his wife & children, or servants, shall be alowed for everie person now aged 16 years & upward, a single share in the devision, or if he provid them necessaries, a duble share, of if they be between 10 year old and 16, then 2 of them to be reconed for a person, both in transportation and devision.

8. That such children as now goe, & are under the age of ten years, have noe other shar in the devision, but 50 acers of unmanured land.

9. That such persons as die before the 7 years be expired, their executors to have their parte or sharr at the devision, proportionably to the time of their life in the collonie.

10. That all such persons as are of this collonie, are to have their meate, drink, apparell, and all provissions out of the common stock & goods of the said collonie'.

It was a tough contract but, since they were so anxious to be gone, the Pilgrims accepted this agreement even though they still believed 'the houses, & lands improved, espetialy gardens & home lotts should remaine undevided wholy to the planters at the 7 years end' and 'that they should have had 2 days in a weeke for their owne private imploymente, for the more comforte of them selves and their families, espetialy such as had families'.

Bradford hoped this demanding contract would become a statement for posterity 'that their children may see with what difficulties their fathers wrastled in going through these things in their first beginnings, and how God brought them along notwithstanding all their weaknesses & infirmities'.

At least now, with the difficult negotiations behind them, they could climb aboard and put to sea on the first leg of the voyage to their promised land.

4 Abandoning a Sinking Ship

July–September 1620

So they lefte that goodly & pleasante
citie, which had been ther resting place
near 12 years; but they knew they were
pilgrimes, & looked not much on those
things, but lift up their eyes to the
heavens, their dearest cuntrie, and
quieted their spirits.

William Bradford

The Pilgrims left Europe at an opportune time. By 1620 the Thirty Years War was well under way, with Catholics and Protestants locked in a violent conflict that would not end till 1648. The Spanish threat materialized in the form of an invasion as troops drove their way further north from the Iberian Peninsula, leaving a trail of destruction and misery behind them.

Because the Dutch dominated international trading routes and the Dutch East India Company itself had thrown a network around the globe, Holland was an ideal departure point. There was no lack of experienced ships' captains or crew for the voyage the Pilgrims now undertook.

July, 1620 Announcing their departure from Holland, Bradford related: 'At length, after much travell and these debats, all things were got ready and provided'. The Pilgrims had been able to charter the *Speedwell*, which Bradford hoped they could use for fishing in the colony when they arrived. The *Speedwell* was smaller than the average size of fishing vessels that worked the coastal waters off Holland and seemed a dangerously small ship in which to sail across the three thousand miles of the Atlantic Ocean to America — especially as so many had died in the previous maritime expedition to Virginia in the ship chartered by Elder Blackwell. Yet they had plans for this ship: 'A smale ship (of some 60 tune) was bought, & fitted in Holand, which was intended as to serve to help to transport them, so to stay in the cuntrie and atend upon fishing and shuch other affairs as might be for the good & benefite of the colonie when they came ther'.

Apart from organizing the ship, Bradford told how, 'The rest of the time was spente in powering out prairs to the Lord with great fervencie, mixed with abundance of tears. And the time being come that they must departe, they were accompanied with most of their brethren out of the citie, unto a towne sundrie miles of called Delfes-Haven, wher the ship lay ready to receive them'.

Bradford related that their departure, although an occasion for sadness, was made easier by the fact that they knew in their hearts that they were Pilgrims on a mission: 'So they lefte that goodly & pleasante citie, which had been ther resting place near 12 years; but they knew they were pilgrimes, (Heb. 11) & looked not much on those things, but lift up their eyes to the heavens, their dearest cuntrie, and quieted their spirits'

21 July   On 21 July, the *Speedwell* was ready to sail out of Delftshaven on the first leg of the epic Pilgrim voyage to America. Delftshaven was a busy port, twenty four miles south of Leyden and two miles southwest of Rotterdam on the north side of the River Maas, not far from the Hook of Holland. 'When they came to the place they found the ship and all things ready; and shuch of their freinds as could not come with them followed after them, and sundrie also came from Amsterdame to see them shipte and to take their leave of them. That night was spent with litle sleepe by the most, but with freindly entertainmente & christian discourse and other reall expressions of true christian love'.

22 July   Captain Reynolds refused to overload his tiny vessel and many Pilgrims were forced to remain behind. Some families had to be divided. Bradford took his wife, Dorothy, but their son stayed in Leyden; Mary Brewster took the two youngest children but left the older ones behind, hoping to connect up with her husband, William, in England en route; but Isaac Allerton was able to take his three children and pregnant wife.

The passenger list of Pilgrims on the initial *Speedwell* voyage — which planned to connect up with the *Mayflower* in England for the final leg to America — included William Bradford and his wife Dorothy; John Carver's wife Katherine, servant John Howland, Mrs Carver's companion Desire Minter and Mrs Carver's maid and servant Roger Wilder; Edward Winslow and his wife Elizabeth, and their servants George Soule and Elias Story; Elder William Brewster and his wife Mary and sons, Love and Wrestling; Isaac Allerton and his wife Mary, their son Bartholomew and daughters Remember and Mary, along with servant boy John Hooke; the Pilgrims' surgeon, Dr Samuel Fuller and his servant, William Button; Captain Myles Standish and his wife Rose; William White and his wife, Susanna, their son Resolved, and servants William Holbeck and Edward Thompson; Deacon Thomas Blossom and

Reverend John Robinson held a special dockside service for his Pilgrims as they left Holland on their voyage to the New World.

his son; Edward Tilley and his wife Ann; John Tilley and his wife Bridget and daughter Elizabeth; John Crackston and his son John; Francis Cooke and his son John; John Turner and his two sons; Digory Priest, Thomas Rogers and his son Joseph; Moses Fletcher; Thomas Williams; Thomas Tinker, his wife and son; Edward Fuller, his wife and their son Samuel; John Rigsdale and his wife Alice; Francis Eaton, his wife and their son, Samuel; Peter Browne; William King; Richard Clarke; John Goodman; Edward Margeson and Richard Britteridge.

It was an historic moment. 'The next day, the wind being faire, they wente aborde, and their freinds with them, where truly dolfull was the sight of that sade and mournfull parting; to see what sighs and sobbs and praires did sound amongst them, what tears did gush from every eye, & pithy speeches peirst each harte; that sundry of the Dutch strangers that stood on the key as spectators, could not refraine from tears. Yet comfortable & sweete it was to see shuch lively and true expressions of dear & unfained love.

Before they left Holland, Robinson farewelled his flock with an appropriate sermon as Bradford related: 'So being ready to departe, they had a day of solleme humiliation, their pastor taking his texte from Ezra 8: 21. *And ther at the river, by Ahava, I proclaimed a fast, that we might humble ourselves before our God, and seeke of him a right way for us, and for our children, and for all our substance.*

'But the tide (which stays for no man) caling them away that were thus loath to departe, there Reved. pastor falling downe on his knees, (and they all with him,) with watrie cheeks commended them with most fervente praiers to the Lord and his blessing. And then with mutuall imbrases and many tears, they tooke their leaves one of an other; which proved to be the last leave to many of them'.

The *Speedwell* enjoyed a 'prosperus winde' sailing out of the canal systems of Holland and then southwest into the English Channel.

23 July   The *Speedwell* sailed southwest down the English Channel and before long they were within sight of the White Cliffs of Dover.

24 July   By now the *Speedwell* was in English coastal waters and sailing along the southern coast of England.

25 July   By the fourth day they were within reach of their destination and waiting for favorable winds with which to enter Southampton waters where they dropped anchor 'wher they found the bigger ship come from London, lying ready, with all the rest of their company'. Bradford confirmed that the *Mayflower* was already chartered as 'Another was hired at London, of burden about 9 score; and all other things gott in readines'.

26 July   Although the *Speedwell* was safely at anchor and the first leg of their voyage successfully completed, it seemed the Pilgrims' problems had only just begun. Bradford: 'After a joyfull wellcome, and mutuall congratulations, with other frendly entertainements, they fell to parley aboute their bussines, how to dispatch with the best expedition; as allso with their agents, about the alteration of the conditions'. This 'parley' actually opened up a can of worms; their agents and investors in London had got cold feet and did not want to put as much money into the charter of the ships, suspecting that the financial potential of the New World expedition was not as lucrative as they had been led to believe. Weston, Carver and Cushman all came on board with a list of problems that threatened to delay, if not abort, the second leg of the voyage to America.

Bradford accused the expedition organizers of inefficiency and deceit: 'Carver pleaded that he knew not well what the other had don at London and Cushman answered, he had done nothing but what he was urged too and it was a good thing he had taken some initiative other wise all had bene dasht and many undon. . . for giveing them notise at Leyden of this change, he could not well in regarde of the shortnes of the time'. So the departure plans bogged down.

31 July   The first round of bickering and betrayal was actually one of the initial tests they had to face without their religious leader John Robinson who had guided them for so many years in Leyden. Fortunately for the confused and bewildered Pilgrims letters soon arrived from Robinson encouraging them to persevere; he wrote that he had a 'true feeling of our perplexitie of mind & toyle of body' but 'the spirite' he hoped would 'sustaine' them.

Robinson obviously felt bad about not sailing with the first groups. He promised he would follow soon saying he wanted to 'assure your selfe that my harte is with you, and that I will not forslowe my bodily coming at the first oppertunitie though I be constrained for a while to be bodily absente from you. I say constrained, God knowing how willingly, & much rather then otherwise, I would have borne my part with you in this first brunt, were I not by strong necessitie held back for the present'.

The main guidelines for the new Pilgrim colony were provided by Robinson, who advised them on constitutional matters, religious activities, social relations and government. While they were sorting out their business problems, the Pilgrims called conferences to listen to continuing letters of advice from Robinson. These included his warning that the religiously motivated Pilgrims had to get along well with the lay pilgrims or 'strangers', telling them to take 'great care' as 'you are many of you strangers, as to the persons, so to the infirmities one of another, & so stand in neede of more watchfullnes this way'.

Robinson wrote, 'let every man represe in him selfe & the whol body in each person, as so many rebels against the commone good'. He recommended they establish a goverement as wisely as possible, and show due respect to their chosen representatives: 'wheras you are become a body politik, using amongst your selves civill govermente, and are not furnished with any persons of spetiall eminencie above the rest, to be chosen by you into office of government, let your wisdome & godlines appeare, not only in chusing shuch persons as doe entirely love and will promote the commone good, but also in yeelding unto them all due honour & obedience in their lawfull administrations'.

2 August Robinson's timely advice was needed by the Pilgrims because they were, even now, battling for survival. The investors and agents had betrayed them by demanding more equity in the venture and a higher proportion from the export sales of the furs and other commodities they anticipated would be sent back to England. But the Pilgrims had had enough and would not be tricked into further exploitation. Bradford wrote: 'Mr. Weston, likewise, came up from London to see them' and asked them to sign the new contract and to have the conditions confirmed; 'but they refused, and answered him, that he knew right well that these were not according to the first agreemente, neither could they yeeld to them without the consente of the rest that were behind. And indeed they had spetiall charge when they came away, from the cheefe of those that were behind, not to doe it. At which he was much offended, and tould them, they must then looke to stand on their owne leggs'.

3 August Bradford related how an angry Weston 'returned in displeasure, and this was the first ground of discontent betweene them'. This led to all sorts of financial problems as their agents now refused to help them pay their accounts; 'And wheras ther wanted well near £100 to clear things away, he would not take order to disburse a penie, but let them shift as they could'.

The Pilgrims were becoming desperate. They had been in the ships for too long already and were so anxious to go that they decided to sell some of their precious food supplies in order to pay their bills: 'So they were forst to selle of some of their provissions to stope this gape, which was some 3 or 4 score firkins of butter, which comoditie they might best spare, being provided too large a quantitie of that kind'.

Yet the revised contract continued to upset them because it asked them to work harder and to share more of their possessions and produce with the investors than they had agreed to do. Bradford wrote: 'We cannot conferr togeather, we thinke it meete (though brefly) to show you the just cause & reason of our differing from those articles last made by Robart Cushman, without our commission or knowledg. And though he might propound good ends to himselfe, yet it no way justifies his doing it'.

Bradford pointed out that the Pilgrims had been looking forward to owning their own homes as 'holding of house and lands; the injoying wheof some of your selves well know, was one spetiall motive, amongst many other, to provoke us to goe'.

The Pilgrims were prepared to promise a generous share of the profits so 'that it may appeare to all men that are not lovers of our selves only, but desire also the good & inriching of our friends who have adventured your moneys with our persons' and 'that if large profits should not arise within the 7 years, that we will continue togeather longer with you'.

But the Pilgrims were determined to set out on their voyage, no matter what the cost was, as Bradford confirmed: 'We are in shuch a streate at presente, as we are forced to sell away £60 worth of our provissions to cleare the Haven, & withall put our selves upon great extremities, scarce haveing any butter, no oyle, not a sole to mend a shoe, nor every man a sword to his side, wanting many muskets, much armoure, &c. And yet we are willing to expose our selves to shuch eminente dangers as are like to insue, & trust to the good providence of God, rather then his name & truth should be evil spoken of for us'.

4 August   Inspired by Robinson's letters of instruction and full of fresh resolve, the Pilgrims paid their bills, made the compromises with the difficult investors by signing the final contract, giving up a greater share of their houses, land and profits, and prepared to leave England forever. Their ranks had swollen by now as new 'strangers' joined their ranks, and different Pilgrims had to be allocated to different ships.

The *Mayflower*, which was now ready to sail was, at 180 tons, the larger of the two ships. She was a three-masted, fully-rigged ship, carrying square sails on each mast and was approximately 90 feet long on deck and 104 feet long overall including the bowspit. She was 78ft 8in at the water line, with a beam of twenty one and a half feet and was owned by a wealthy merchant of London, Thomas Goffe, who was commercially involved with the investors and who was an intimate friend and business associate of John Winthrop who was to help found the colony of Massachusetts within ten years. The *Mayflower* had been built in the Leigh-on-Sea shipyards in the late sixtenth century and had been used to carry cargoes of cloth to France and wine back to England as one of the many commercial 'sweet ships'. For her voyage to America her skipper was Captain Christopher Jones who also had a share in the ownership.

Most of the Pilgrims wanted to travel on the *Mayflower* as it was the larger and more comfortable ship, but the leaders decided to allocate places on the different ships. Some who had come across from Holland in the *Speedwell* were transferred to the *Mayflower*, while others were transferred across to the *Speedwell*. 'Then they ordered & distributed their company for either shipe, as they conceived for the best'.

The Captains of the different ships, fearing confusion, then announced that the time had come to select ship leaders and assistants, so Bradford wrote they 'chose a Govenor & 2 or 3 assistants for each shipe, to order the people by the way, and see to the dispossing of there provissions, and shuch like affairs. All which was not only with the liking of the maisters of the ships, but according to their desires'.

5 August Expecting this to be their moment of departure from the Old World Bradford related that at last 'they sett sayle from thence about the 5 of August'.

And so the two little ships set out from the bustling Hampshire port of Southampton and headed southwest for the Atlantic. Even though the Pilgrims were relieved to be underway at last, it must have been an emotional time for them; they were turning their back on their original homes and literally casting their bread on the waters.

6 August The two ships *Mayflower* and the *Speedwell* sailed on making their way through baffling winds down the Solent, heading southwest.

7 August Sailing across Lyme Bay, both ships made reasonable progress as they sailed past Lyme Regis and Bournemouth.

8 August Luck was not on the side of the Pilgrims, however. By the time the ships were sailing past Weymouth, the *Speedwell* began showing signs of leaking; water had begun to trickle in through the timbers of the hull. As Bradford wrote, the situation was serious: 'Being thus put to sea they had not gone farr, but Mr. Reinolds the master of the leser ship complained that he found his ship so leak as he durst not put further to sea till she was mended'.

9 August With the ships crossing Lyme Bay, the *Speedwell* now began to leak badly as the timbers, now soaked, let in an increasing flow of water. It required almost constant pumping. The Pilgrims were alarmed. Here was the first portent about *Speedwell's* lack of suitability for the Atlantic crossing.

10 August Not long after the ships passed Dartmouth, the gravity of the situation became apparent. *Speedwell* was leaking even worse by now and the pumps were unable to cope. Both ships were ordered to heave to for a conference between the Captains and the Pilgrim leaders. They decided that the ships should turn back for Dartmouth, the nearest convenient port. As Bradford said, an inspection would have to be carried out before the *Speedwell* could be repaired: 'So the master of the biger ship (caled Mr. Jonas) being consulted with, they both resolved to put into Dartmouth & have her ther searched & mended'.

12 August   Eventually the *Mayflower* and the crippled *Speedwell* managed to sail into the safety of Dartmouth Harbor and drop anchor. Bradford related that this was at no small cost to the Pilgrims, already a long way behind schedule, as the ships were now docked 'to their great charg & losse of time and a faire winde'.

13 August   The Pilgrims waited on board while Captain Reynolds of the *Speedwell* attempted to organize repairs to his ship.

14 August   Cargo was moved around on the *Speedwell* so that she could be over-hauled and retrimmed in a thorough manner. Bradford says she was 'thorowly searcht from steme to sterne'.

15 August   The ship's hull was found to be badly in need of repair and 'some leakes were found & mended'.

17 August   The Pilgrims resolve was being damaged by this waiting period. The delays and unseaworthy ships were proving too much for the more faint-hearted. The first Pilgrim of any substance to cause trouble was the uncertain and sickly Robert Cushman, who was now having second thoughts about even going to America. He wrote from Dartmouth to a friend, 'For besids the eminente dangers of this viage, which are no less then deadly, an infirmitie of body hath ceased me, which will not in all licelyhoode leave me till death'.

Cushman had been frightened by the sinking ship. He claimed that the *Speedwell* 'will not cease leaking, els I thinke we had been halfe way at Virginia' and complained that 'our viage hither hath been as full of crosses, as our selves have been of crokednes'. He believed the *Speedwell* would have sunk because the gaps in the timbers were so wide 'if we had stayed at sea but 3 or 4 howers more, shee would have sunke right downe. And though she was twise trimmed at Hampton, yet now shee is open and leakie as a seive; and ther was a borde, a man might have puld of with his fingers, 2 foote longe, where the water came in as at a mole hole'.

The Pilgrims were now in trouble. They could only afford limited food supplies and 'Our victualls will be halfe eaten up, I thinke, before we goe from the coaste of England, and if our viage last longe, we shall not have a months victialls when we come in the countrie'. The Pilgrim leaders were also upsetting their own people by now, because they would not let them get off the ships for fear that they would never come back. Cushman actually attacked his *Speedwell* ship leader Christopher Martin: 'he so insulteth over our poore people, with shuch scorne & contempte, as if they were not good enough to wipe his shoes. It would break your hart to see his dealing'. And if Cushman asked for favors on behalf of the other Pilgrims, he claimed Martin 'flies in my face, as mutinous, and saith no complaints shall be heard or received but by

The arms of the Merchant Adventurers.

GOD BE OVR FRIEND

Arms of the Merchants. Although mainly a commercial operation the Arms of the Merchant Adventurers, who funded the Mayflower *voyage, also had its own religious motto.*

him selfe, and saith they are forwarde, & waspish, discontented people, & I doe ill to hear them ... he will not hear them, nor suffer them to goe ashore, least they should rune away'.

Everything had gone wrong according to Cushman who described the investors as 'bloudsuckers' who had betrayed them 'and felt they would all become slaves'. He concluded with a pessimistic prophecy: 'Freind, if ever we make a plantation, God works a mirakle; especially considering how scante we shall be of victualls, and most of all ununited amongst our selves, & devoyed of good tutors & regimente. Violence will break all. Wher is the meek & humble spirite of Moyses & of Nehemiah who reedified the wals of Jerusalem, & the state of Isreaell' and 'Have not the philosophers and all wise men observed that, even in setled commone welths, violente governours bring either them selves, or people, or boath to ruine; how much more in the raising of commone wealths, when the morter is yet scarce tempered that should bind the wales'.

By now Cushman believed that if they did not die at sea they would starve: 'I see not in reason how we shall escape even the gasping of hunger starved persons' and 'we can not guess who shall be meate first for the fishes'. In this desperate vein he swore 'That which I have writen is treue' and 'I write it as upon my life, and last confession in England' as 'my head is weake, & my body feeble'.

21 August   The overhauling of the *Speedwell* was completed and the cargo was replaced.

22 August   Once again the Pilgrims prepared themselves to set out on their epic voyage, Bradford recorded patiently: 'and now it was conceived by the workmen & all, that she was sufficiente, & they might proceede without either fear or danger'.

23 August   The Pilgrims now left England for America for the second time. 'So with good hopes from hence, they put to sea againe, conceiving they should goe comfortably on, not looking for any more lets of this kind'.

24 August   Both the *Speedwell* and the *Mayflower* sailed west-southwest from Dartmouth along the coast of England, heading towards the Atlantic and enjoyed a fair wind.

25 August   Unbelievably, even as the fair winds picked up and the two ships gathered speed for their run to America, the *Speedwell* was reported to be leaking again.

26 August   Although the ships were now 100 leagues or 300 miles southwest of Lands End and well on their way to the Atlantic crossing, the *Speedwell* was now leaking dangerously. They had hoped that this would be a successful voyage but 'it fell out otherwise, for after they were gone to sea againe above 100 leagues without the Lands End, houlding company togeather all this while, the master of the small ship complained his ship was so leake as he must bear up or sinke at sea, for they could scarce free her with much pumping'.

There was no alternative but to turn back. 'So they came to consultation againe, and resolved both ships to bear up backe againe & put into Plimmoth, which accordingly was done'.

27 August   Both ships sailed back for England, this time making for Plymouth Harbor.

28 August   Once in Plymouth Harbor, arrangements were made to have the *Speedwell* examined yet again, 'But no spetiall leake could be found, but it was judged to be the general weaknes of the shipe, and that shee would not prove sufficiente for the voiage'.

29 August   After lengthy discussions, the Captains of the two ships and the Pilgrim leaders decided to take the radical step of dividing their fleet in half, leaving the *Speedwell* behind and setting out for America in the *Mayflower* alone. Bradford reported: 'Upon which it was resolved to dismise her & parte of the companie, and proceede with the other shipe. The which (though it was greevous, & caused great discouragemente) was put in execution'.

30 August   The Pilgrims quickly transferred cargo from the *Speedwell* to the *Mayflower* and began the task of deciding who was going to stay behind in England and who was going to go to America.

1 September   The Pilgrim leaders then selected the people to go in the *Mayflower* and asked the remaining numbers to return to London. The different groups collected their possessions and prepared to go their separate ways: one group back to London and historical obscurity, the others to America to write their names in history.

2 September   A rather relieved Robert Cushman returned with the *Speedwell* group to London and dry land — having written his last 'will and testament' two weeks earlier beause he was expecting to die at sea. Bradford claimed that the 'hart & courage' of Pilgrims like Cushman 'was gone from them before' as soon as they sailed into the first trouble.

Bradford claims that many of the group remaining behind were in fact relieved rather than disappointed. The leaking ship had provided them with an opportunity of sorting out the chaff from the grain. 'So after they had tooke out such provission as the other ship could well stow, and concluded both what number and what persons to send bak, they made another sad parting, the one ship going backe for London, and the other was to proceede on her viage. Those that went bak were for the most parte such as were willing so to doe, either out of some discontente, or fear they conceived of the ill success of the vioage, seeing so many croses befale, & the year time so farr spente; but others, in regarde of their owne weaknes, and charge of many yonge children, were thought least usefull, and most unfite to bear the brunte of this hard adventure; unto which worke of God and judgmente of their brethern, they were contented to submite. And thus, like Gedions armie, this small number was devided, as if the Lord by this worke of his providence thought these few to many for the great worke he had to doe'.

3 September Bradford then revealed a scandal concerning the leaking *Speedwell*. Although it appeared the ship was not seaworthy — because apart from leaking she was heavily overmasted — the real problem lay with the dishonesty of the crew. From research that he was able to do sub-sequently, Bradford claimed that the ship's Captain and crew lied to the Pilgrims by pretending that the ship was leaking and creating temporary holes in the hull. He claimed that they did this so that they could get out of going to America where they feared the *Mayflower* crew would eat all the food (as the *Mayflower* carried all the victuals) and they would die of starvation: 'by the cuning & deceite of the master & his company, who were hired to stay a whole year in the cuntrie, and now fancying dislike & fearing wante of victeles, they ploted this strategem to free them selves; as afterwards was knowne, & by some of them confessed. For they apprehended that the greater ship, being of force, & in whom most of the provissions were stowed, she would retayne enough for her selfe, what soever became of them or the passengers'.

4 September The *Speedwell* weighed anchor and sailed back to London with Cushman and others on board, leaving the *Mayflower* and the colonizing party in Plymouth.

5 September With the troublesome *Speedwell* out of the way the Pilgrims now concentrated on last-minute preparations to equip the *Mayflower* for the two month sea voyage. By nightfall she was ready to sail on the first tide after first light the following morning.

6 September Once again the Pilgrims set out for America.

With false starts behind them and the faint-hearted weeded out of the colonizing party, the survivors now gritted their teeth and put to sea.

This was their third attempt and as it turned out it was to be third time lucky. Without the ill-fated *Speedwell* holding her back the sturdy *Mayflower* weighed anchor, dropped her canvas and sailed out of Plymouth Harbor towards the Atlantic, bound at last for the northern coast of Virginia.

The epic *Mayflower* voyage had finally begun.

5 Voyage of the Mayflower

September–November 1620

'But it plased God before they came halfe
seas over, to smite this yong man with a
greeveous disease, of which he dyed in a
desperate maner, and so was him selfe
the first that was throwne overbord.'

William Bradford

6 September

The Pilgrims hoped to reach America within eight weeks. None of them had any idea how violent the seas of the Atlantic Ocean could be and how much their ship would be tossed about. None of them had ever undertaken a major voyage before. The longest trip for most of them had been the channel crossing from England to Holland. With its thousands of miles of open seas the Atlantic must have seemed terrifying to the Pilgrims huddled together in their little ship.

The *Mayflower* voyage started out well enough, even if their departure meant leaving some good friends behind. Winslow described how they 'loosed from Ploymouth; having been kindly intertained and courteously used by divers friends there dwelling'. Bradford added optimistically that their 'troubls being blowne over, and now all being compacte togeather in one shipe' at last 'they put to sea againe with a prosperus winde'.

In all, the *Mayflower* group now totalled 102 passengers. They crowded the little vessel with another twenty five people. These were members of the ship's crew. All were squeezed into the hold below decks and the various cabins, and such nooks and crannies as the long boat (or shallop) in which some of them slept.

Perhaps realizing the significance of this epic moment, Bradford listed in family groups the names of this first shipload of Pilgrims. He said there were 'about a hundred sowls' who 'came over in this first ship'.

In this most authoritative list of all Bradford wrote these were 'the names of those which came over first, in the year 1620, and were by the

William Bradford. Oil. Anon. Flemish school. Reproduced by kind
permission of Melbourne collector.

Edward Winslow. Oil. Anon. Reproduced by kind permission of Pilgrim Hall, Plymouth, Massachusetts, USA.

Captain Myles Standish. Oil by Daniel Mytens, Flemish school. Reproduced by kind permission of National Geographic Society, Washington, USA.

The Mayflower *and the hapless* Speedwell *riding at anchor in Dartmouth Harbor*. Oil by Leslie Wilcox. Reproduced by kind permission of Pilgrim Hall, Plymouth, Massachusetts, USA.

The tiny Mayflower *tossed by the Atlantic. It was such a harrowing voyage for the Pilgrims that they were fortunate to lose only one of their number at sea.* Oil by Marshall W. Joyce. Reproduced by kind permission of Plymouth Plantation, Plymouth, Massachusetts, USA.

Plymouth Rock. The first landing place on a frozen shoreline for a desperate group. Oil by Henry Botkin. Reproduced by kind permission of Pilgrim Hall, Massachusetts, USA.

Despite an initial skirmish, the Pilgrims and the Indians established a workable relationship at first; unfortunately, it did not last for too many years. Oil. Anon. Reproduced by kind permission of Pilgrim Hall, Plymouth, Massachusetts, USA.

After the first terrible winter, the spring harvest proved so plentiful that the Pilgrims thanked their Lord with an extravagant thanksgiving celebration which is celebrated to this day. Oil by Jennie Brownscombe. Reproduced by kind permission of Pilgrim Hall, Plymouth, Massachusetts, USA.

Company seal. Most of the trading companies of the day had their own seal.

blessing of God the first beginers and (in a sort) the foundation of all the Plantations and Colonies in New-England; and their families.

'Mr. John Carver; Kathrine, his wife; Desire Minter; & 2 man-servants; John Howland; Roger Wilder; William Latham, a boy; & a maid servant, & a child that was put to him, called Jasper More.

'Mr. William Brewster; Mary, his wife; with 2 sons, whose names were Love and Wrasling; and a boy was put to him called Richard More; and another of his brothers. The rest of his children were left behind, & came over afterwards.

'Mr. Edward Winslow; Elizabeth, his wife; & 2 men servants, caled Georg Sowle and Elias Story; also a litle girle was put to him, caled Ellen, the sister of Richard More.

'William Bradford, and Dorothy, his wife; having but one child, a sone, left behind, who came afterward.

'Mr. Isaack Allerton, and Mary, his wife; with 3 children, Bartholmew, Remember, & Mary; and a servant boy, John Hooke.

'Mr. Samuell Fuller, and a servant, caled William Butten. His wife was behind, & a child, which came afterwards.

'John Crakston, and his sone, John Crakston.

'Captin Myles Standish, and Rose.

'Mr. Christopher Martin, and his wife, and 2. servants, Salamon Prower and John Langemore.

'Mr. William Mullines, and his wife, and 2 children, Joseph & Priscila; and a servant, Robart Carter.

'Mr. William White, and Susana, his wife, and one sone, caled Resolved, and one borne a ship-bord, caled Peregriene; & 2 servants, named William Holbeck & Edward Thomson.

'Mr. Steven Hopkins, & Elizabeth, his wife, and 2 children, caled Giles, and Constanta, a doughter, both by a former wife; and 2 more by this wife, caled Damaris & Oceanus: the last was borne at sea; and 2 servants, called Edward Doty and Edward Litster.

'Mr. Richard Warren; but his wife and children were lefte behind, and came afterwards.

'John Billinton, and Elen, his wife; and 2 sones, John & Francis.

'Edward Tillie, and Ann, his wife; and 2 children that were their cossens, Henery Samson and Humillity Coper.

'John Tillie, and his wife; and Eelizabeth, their doughter.

'Francis Cooke, and his sone John. But his wife & other children came afterwards.

'Thomas Rogers, and Joseph his sone. His other children came afterwards.

'Thomas Tinker, and his wife, and a sone.

'John Rigdale, and Alice, his wife.

'James Chilton, and his wife, and Mary, their doughter. They had an other doughter, that was maried, came afterward.

'Edward Fuller, and his wife, and Samuell, their sonne.

Despite its historic role, the Mayflower *was a typical commercial vessel of the period.*

'John Turner, and 2 sones. He had a doughter came some years after to Salem, wher she is now living.

'Francis Eaton, and Sarah, his wife, and Samuell, their sone, a yong child.

'Moyses Fletcher, John Goodman, Thomas Williams, Digerie Preist, Edmond Margeson, Peter Browne, Richard Britterige, Richard Clarke, Richard Gardenar, Gilbart Winslow.

'John Alden was hired for a cooper, at South-Hampton, wher the ship vituled; and being a hopfull yong man, was much desired, but left to his owne liking to go or stay when he came here; but he stayed, and maryed here.

'John Allerton and Thomas Enlish were both hired......But they both dyed here, before the shipe returned.'

On top of this first shipload of Pilgrims, Bradford added two extra hired hands who helped in Plymouth for a while but then 'returned when their time was out: William Trevore (a seaman hired to stay a year) and Ely (a seaman hired to stay a year).

7 September

Because of the delays the *Mayflower* left England weeks later than her skipper would have wished. Now, instead of crossing the Atlantic in summer, he was faced with a fall voyage which he knew could be fraught with storms. For such a small ship it was a long way. To cross the ocean the skipper would have sailed southwest to pick up favorable winds and currents and escape the colder conditions before heading northwest again as he aproached the north American coastline. But it was a great distance; he was leaving Plymouth which is located on Longitude 4 degrees west and had to sail across the Atlantic to the North American coast making a landfall at Cape Cod on Longitude 70 degrees west — an epic voyage which, although it was not recorded closely at the time, would have followed a course something like that reconstructed here.

To start with it seems the Pilgrims were lucky. With favorable winds Captain Jones was able to set all the *Mayflower*'s sails once she cleared Plymouth Harbor. She then sailed past the dangerous Eddystone Rock and southwest out to sea. Then she settled into some steady sailing; the good winds 'continued diverce days togeather, which was some incouragmente unto them' even through before long the winds whipped up into something of a gale.

8 September

Fortunately favorable east-northeast winds continued to blow the little *Mayflower* along the southwest coast of England and past the Lizard Point with the strength of a moderate gale that the ship could handle.

9 September

The gale strength winds continued and with most sails set the ship made good progress passing the landmark of Lands End after which the swells increased and 'according to the usuall maner many were afflicted with sea-sicknes'.

10 September	With the gale continuing the ship was now well beyond Lands End and, as this was Sunday, the Pilgrims gave thanks in a specially heartfelt prayer meeting.
11 September	The *Mayflower* sailed further away from the main coast of England south of the last piece of English land mass, the Scilly Isles.
12 September	The Pilgrims had now been a week at sea. At this stage they were approaching Longitude 10 degrees west. Bradford says that the favorable conditions then bore them rapidly out of sight of the land they so loved, and continued until they were near the middle of the Atlantic.
13 September	Enjoying favorable east-northeast winds, the *Mayflower* sailed deeper into the Atlantic on a course that would take it on a line about halfway between the Azores and Iceland and then some weeks later below the bottom of the tip of Greenland and finally under Newfoundland to the coast of North America.
14 September	Many of the Pilgrims now had their sea legs and were moving more freely about the ship.
15 September	Different members of the group reorganized their quarters and the leaders decided on more permanent places for the different family groups.
16 September	The crew were becoming irritated by the Pilgrims who were spending more time moving about the ship and quarrels began to occur.
17 September	Prayer services were held to mark the Sabbath with appropriate bible readings from Elder William Brewster.
18 September	As they became more confident of their position on the ship the Pilgrims took the opportunity to dry their wet clothes by hanging them on the rigging.
19 September	The Pilgrims had now been two weeks at sea. The *Mayflower* had sailed across the ocean as far as Longitude 15 degrees west and, although hundreds of miles south, was directly below the east tip of Iceland.
20 September	Captain Jones, handling increasing complaints from his crew, now asked the Pilgrims to keep to their quarters as much as possible. Of course, by now their living areas below decks were stagnant and smelt. The seas were too rough for the ship's hatches to be opened during the day and — as they had to sleep, eat, retch and defecate in buckets below decks — the atmosphere had become putrid. They were forced to seek fresh air on the main deck whenever possible, and this in turn

had irritated the crew who were busy enough tying and untying the scores of ropes needed to furl and unfurl the sails.

Bradford complained that, led by a 'profane' and 'lustie yonge man', the *Mayflower* sailors now began to tease and taunt their religious passengers at every opportunity.

21 September

Despite the sailors' opposition, the Pilgrims tried to dry their bedding and other clothes that were getting increasingly wet from the seas that broke over the gunwales and seeped through the decking into their quarters.

22 September

As they sailed further out into the Atlantic, some of the Pilgrims began to get seasick again and also became frightened as the seas increased. This irritated the impatient sailors even further.

23 September

Ships like the Mayflower *featured the colors of the company responsible for the charter.*

Just when Bradford considered the quarrels between the sailors and the Pilgrims were reaching boiling point, the Pilgrims experienced what he saw as the hand of Providence. 'Ther was a proud & very profane yonge man, one of the sea-men, of a lustie, able body, which made him the more hauty; he would allway be contemning the poore people in their sicknes, & cursing them dayly with greevous execrations, and did not let to tell them, that he hoped to help to cast halfe of them over board before they came to their jurneys end, and to make mery with what they had; and if he were by any gently reproved, he would curse and swear most bitterly'.

This 'yonge man' was unable to toss any Pilgrims over the side of the *Mayflower* however as 'it plased God before they came halfe seas over, to smite this yong man with a greeveous disease, of which he dyed in a desperate maner, and so was him selfe the first that was throwne overbord. Thus his curses light on his owne head; and it was an astonishmente to all his fellows, for they noted it to be the just hand of God upon him'. Bradford saw this as 'a spetiall worke of Gods providence'.

24 September

Prayer services were held to thank God for their deliverance from such evils and for general safe progress.

25 September

Conditions began to get rough and they began to feel the impact of high seas of the mid-Atlantic in the fall.

26 September

The Pilgrims had now been at sea for three weeks. The *Mayflower* had sailed across the Atlantic to Longitude 20 degrees west and was level with central Iceland.

27 September

The high seas and stronger winds were proving too much for the little *Mayflower*. It now appeared as if she might collapse under the strain, because one of the most important structural supports, the main beam, began to split open. Bradford explained: 'After they had injoyed faire winds and weather for a season, they were incountred many times with crosse winds, and mette with many feirce stormes, with which the shipe was shroudly shaken, and her upper works made very leakie; and one of the maine beames in the midd ships was bowed & craked, which put them in some fear that the shipe could not be able to performe the vioage'.

With the main beam cracked the ship was in real danger. For a time it looked as if they could all go to their watery graves or at least that the expedition might have to be cancelled. Memories of the 130 dead on Francis Blackwell's ships haunted them as they discussed the alternatives.

28 September

Although the Mayflower *experienced many high seas during its nine-week voyage, the Pilgrims never lost faith in their mission.*

Nobody knew what to do. Captain Jones had the sails hauled in and tied down and organized a discussion in the bowels of the little ship while she tossed around in the stormy mid-Atlantic hundreds of miles from the nearest land. He asked his officers and men but they all disagreed as to what to do. Some wanted to turn back rather than risk drowning but others wanted to go forward because otherwise they would lose their wages. The ship however may not last long enough above water to go forward or back, as even as they spoke the main beam was splitting further and further.

Bradford listened in on this desperate conference and recorded: 'Some of the cheefe of the company, perceiveing the mariners to fear the suffisiencie of the shipe, as appeared by their mutterings, they entred into serious consultation with the master & other officers of the ship, to consider in time of the danger; and rather to returne then to cast them selves into a desperate & inevitable perill'. Fortunately for the Pilgrims the thought of earning increased wages spurred another more influential group of sailors to vote to continue the voyage. Although 'truly ther was great distraction & differance of opinion amongst the mariners them selves' these more daring sailors recommended that 'they doe what could be done for their wages sake, (being now halfe the seas over)'.

29 September

One of the 'miracles' that seemed to accompany the Pilgrims then occurred. Although the Captain did not have a replacement beam, the Pilgrims fortunately happened to have brought some tools and equipment of their own that could be adapted in this situation. The general condition of the hull was considered by the Captain good enough to proceed: 'in examening of all opinions, the master and others affirmed they knew the ship to be strong & firme under water'.

So Captain Jones agreed to try and repair the main beam with the large iron press which the Pilgrims had brought for printing pamphlets in the colony. This was a device in the form of a frame with an iron base at either end and a central screw which ran from one end to the other, enabling the two ends to be screwed tighter together or further apart. By putting this under the main beam and screwing they were able to lift up the base of the main beam like a jack and to slip under it a better, stronger post. This provided a solid foundation for the beam for the rest of the voyage until a new piece of timber could be cut in America. Bradford: 'For the buckling of the maine beame, ther was a great iron scrue the passengers brought out of Holland, which would raise the beame into his place; the which being done, the carpenter & master affirmed that with a post put under it, set firme in the lower deck, & otherways bounde, he would make it sufficiente'.

30 September   These repairs having been completed Bradford says the Captain then agreed to plug the leaks that were allowing water in and slowing the ship down: 'And as for the decks & uper workes they would calke them as well as they could, and though with the workeing of the ship they would not longe keepe stanch, yet ther would otherwise be no great danger, if they did not overpress her with sails'.

Thus through ingenuity and good fortune the mid-Atlantic crisis was averted and instead of aborting their mission yet again 'they commited them selves to the will of God, & resolved to proseede'.

1 October   No sooner had they agreed to proceed when another disaster struck — and this one would have resulted in the loss of one of the more valuable Pilgrims had it not been for yet another piece of good fortune. While they were repairing the ship, storms continued to batter the little vessel; 'And in one of them, as they thus lay at hull, in a mighty storme, a lustie yonge man (called John Howland) coming upon some occasion above the grattings, was, with a seele of the shipe throwne in the sea; but it pleased God that he caught hould of the top-saile halliards, which hunge over board, & rane out at length; yet he held his hould (though he was sundrie fathomes under water) till he was hald up by the same rope to the brime of the water, and then with a boat hooke & other means got into the shipe againe, & his life saved; and though he was something ill with it, yet he lived many years after, and became a profitable member both in church & commone wealthe'.

4 October   The Pilgrims had now been at sea for four long weeks. There had been crisis after crisis but they had survived the crisis with the crew, weathered all storms, repaired the ship and pulled one of their number from the ocean. There seemed to be no stopping them now. Besides, the *Mayflower* had now crossed the Atlantic to Longitude 25 degrees west and was on a line between the Azores and the west coast of Greenland.

5 October   They set off again but had to haul in the sails from time to time for fear of being blown over or having the main beam cracked again as the winds belted all that canvas about. Bradford reported: 'In sundrie of these stormes the winds were so feirce, & the seas so high, as they could not beare a knote of saile, but were forced to hull, for diverce days togither'.

6 October   Storms continued forcing the little *Mayflower* to sit tight and ride out the waves.

7 October   Elizabeth Hopkins, wife of Master Stephen Hopkins, gave birth to a son who, in honor of the circumstances of his birth, was named Oceanus. He was the first child born on board the *Mayflower*, and the only child born on high seas.

Now there were 103 Pilgrims setting out for America.

8 October   With the new baby well-wrapped up against the seas breaking into the ship, the *Mayflower* pressed on. She was setting more sails to catch favorable winds.

9 October   The leaks increased despite the new caulking and it was by now impossible for the Pilgrims to keep dry.

10 October   The Sunday prayer service was held despite the cramped conditions. Elder William Brewster gave thanks for the new born child and their progress across the Atlantic.

11 October   The Pilgrims had been at sea for five weeks and the *Mayflower* had now crossed the Atlantic Ocean as far as Longitude 40 degrees west. So far they had weathered all the storms without losing any of the passengers. In fact, their number had grown from 102 to 103 through the birth of Oceanus. Even so, high seas and following winds tossed the ship about and kept the Pilgrims wet.

12 October   The *Mayflower* had now reached a point that was on a line below Greenland and those on board could take heart at her progress.

13 October   The water splashing into the ship extinguished the galley fires. With no heat for cooking, the Pilgrims had to eat cold food.

14 October   Again many of the Pilgrims were wet through with little chance of drying their clothes and some began to fall sick.

15 October   Some of the Pilgrims began to despair and became depressed due to the long period away from the sight of land. A general state of melancholy had set in.

16 October   The wet and soggy food was becoming monotonous and some of the Pilgrims began to complain of a general feeling of weakness. Early signs of scurvy were setting in.

17 October	In their Sunday prayer service the Pilgrims asked God for patience and courage to continue the arduous voyage.
18 October	The Pilgrims had now been at sea for six weeks. The *Mayflower* had crossed the Atlantic Ocean to Longitude 47 degrees West.
	There was certainly no turning back now no matter how weak some of the Pilgrims felt or how depressed they were.
19 October	By now the tiny *Mayflower* was like a foul prison. Without fresh air or the chance to really clean out their quarters (because everything was so tightly packed) their quarters below had become filthy and smelly. This in turn began to make more of them feel sick. They yearned to reach their promised land.
20 October	Attempts by Captain Jones to set his course for the area north of Virginia were by now increasingly frustrated by winds that began to blow the ship on a more northerly course.
21 October	With little knowledge of their position or sea conditions the patience of many of the Pilgrims by now had worn thin. They looked to their bibles for reassurance.
22 October	Their wet clothes, inadequate food and cramped conditions created frictions between the Pilgrims who were by now getting on each other's nerves — just as Reverend John Robinson had predicted in his farewell letters of advice.
23 October	The daily routine of preparing meals, reading the bible, tidying up the quarters and discussing the position of the ship had by now become monotonous. It was relieved only by accidents as the ship tossed and turned and sent possessions flying about the hold and living quarters.
24 October	The regular Sunday prayer service was used by the Pilgrims to bolster their faith as the days at sea dragged on.
25 October	The Pilgrims had now been at sea for seven weeks. The *Mayflower* had crossed the ocean as far as Longitude 54 degrees West which was on a line with the east tip of New Foundland.
26 October	Wet through for days at a time in the cold Atlantic Ocean the health of the Pilgrims deteriorated further.
27 October	Captain Jones began to worry about his position being further north than he had planned to be at this stage of the voyage.
28 October	Older Pilgrims like John Carver began to spend more time in their bunks, too weak to battle with the motion of the ship any longer.

29 October   The *Mayflower* began to enter a different area of ocean where sea patterns and waves indicated she was nearing the western side of the Atlantic.

30 October   Captain Jones and his officers began to look out for land birds, plants or tree branches blown out to sea and other signs of the approaching coast.

31 October   No trace of any land could be seen by a worried captain and crew. More Pilgrims were falling sick.

1 November   The Pilgrims had now been at sea for two months. The *Mayflower* had crossed the Atlantic to Longitude 63 degrees west.

2 November   The length of time at sea and the poor food struck down an increasing number of Pilgrims. They were now desperate for a sight of land and aware of the tragedy that hit Blackwell's shipload of religious refugees in a similar situation.

3 November   The ordeal had proved too much for William Button, the young servant of Doctor Samuel Fuller. He now fell ill and was put to bed.

4 November   The weather became fine with the seas abating as they approached the coast, but Button remained desperately ill.

5 November   Fine weather continued but Button faded further causing all Pilgrims to intensify their prayers for the Doctor's young servant.

6 November   Despite their prayers the first of the Pilgrims died. Young William Button failed to respond to any of the remedies of his master. Weakened by the long sea voyage, stricken by scurvy and possibly other chest complaints, he breathed his last just before they sighted the promised land for which he had risked so much.

   A saddened Bradford explains: 'In all this viage ther died but one of the passengers, which was William Butten, a youth, servant to Samuell Fuller, when they drew near the coast'.

7 November   The Captain and officers buried William Button by sliding his body over the side. Elder Brewster administered the last rites.

8 November   The Pilgrims had now been at sea for nine weeks. The *Mayflower* had crossed the Atlantic to the North American coastline located on Longitude 70 degrees west. She was within reach of her goal now and all the Pilgrims must have taken heart. Definite signs of land were now being seen. Twigs, land birds and coastal seaweed confirmed that they were almost at their landfall.

   They had hoped to be in north Virginia but contrary winds had blown them far north. By now they were so exhausted that they were prepared to make a landfall wherever they could; even though the first land they saw turned out to be Cape Cod, way to the north of their destination.

9 November The Pilgrims at last actually saw land. Winslow described that after many difficulties in boisterous storms, on 9 November following break of the day, they spied land which they deemed to be Cape Cod ... 'so goodly a land, and wooded to the brink of the sea'.

As official scribe Bradford added: 'After long beating at sea they fell with that land which is called Cape Cod; the which being made & certainly knowne to be it, they were not a litle joyfull'.

10 November Bradford then explained how, even though they realized they were north of the area where they had planned to land, they decided to settle around Cape Cod: 'After some deliberation had amongst them selves & with the master of the ship, they tacked aboute and resolved to stande for the southward (the wind & weather being faire) to finde some place aboute Hudsons river for their habitation. But after they had sailed that course aboute halfe the day, they fell amongst deangerous shoulds and roring breakers, and they were so farr intangled ther with as they conceived them selves in great danger; & the wind shrinking upon them withall, they resolved to bear up againe for the Cape, and thought them selves hapy to gett out of those dangers before night overtooke them, as by Gods providence they did. And the next day they gott into the Cape-harbor wher they ridd in saftie'.

11 November Bradford: 'Being thus arived in a good harbor and brought safe to land, they fell upon their knees & blessed the God of heaven, who had brought them over the vast & furious ocean, and delivered them from all the periles & miseries therof, againe to set their feete on the firme and stable earth, their proper elemente. And no marvell if they were thus joyefull'.

Having sailed thousands of miles across the Atlantic the plucky little *Mayflower* had thus arrived safely in America, finally delivering the Pilgrims to their promised land.

But their joy would be shortlived, for death lay in wait for them on the icy shore. By the end of their first winter half of those now waiting expectantly in the ship would be dead.

6 Gunfight at Eastham Corral

November–December 1620

> *Presently, all on the sudain, they heard a*
> *great & strange crie, which they knew to*
> *be the same voyces they heard in the*
> *night, though they varied their notes, &*
> *one of their company being abroad came*
> *runing in, & cried, "Men, Indeans,*
> *Indeans"; and withall, their arowes*
> *came flying amongst them.*
>
> William Bradford

11 November   The *Mayflower* had landed the Pilgrims safely in America, but she had left England much later than planned and the voyage had taken much longer than it should have. Instead of arriving at a more hospitable time, the North American landscape that now greeted them was a cold and desolate wilderness. It would hardly have seemed a promised land to the little band standing on the deck of their little ship. The thought of carving a home out of this icy wasteland must have seemed daunting especially as the Atlantic storms and shortages of food and water had already weakened their health and tested their resolve.

Bradford, once again aware of the historic moment, summed up their trepidation: 'But hear I cannot but stay and make a pause, and stand half amased at this poore peoples presente condition; and so I thinke will the reader too, when he well considers the same. Being thus passed the vast ocean, and a sea of troubles before in their preparation (as may be remembered by that which wente before), they had now no friends to wellcome them, nor inns to entertaine or refresh their weatherbeaten bodys, no houses or much less townes to repaire too, to seeke for succoure'.

Always mindful of their religious mission as the chosen or transplanted people — 'the vine of Israel' — Bradford then compared their plight with more fortunate biblical refugees who were befriended by local savages: saying 'It is recorded in scripture as a mercie to the apostle & his shipwrake'd company, that "the barbarous people shewed no litle kindness: for they kindled a fire, and received us every one, because of the present rain, and because of the cold"'.

The seal of the New England colony (Nova Anglia) featured an Indian saying 'Come over and help' — unfortunately printed backwards.

But Bradford then claimed that those biblical refugees were luckier with the natives than his Pilgrim group in America as 'these savage barbarians, when they mette with them (as after will appeare) were readier to fill their sids full of arrows then otherwise'.

Bradford in fact believed that the Pilgrims were in something of a predicament. He seemed now to be having second thoughts as everything seemed to be going against the exhausted *Mayflower* voyagers. They could not have come to America at a worse time: 'it was winter, and they that know the winters of that cuntrie know them to be sharp & violent, & subjecte to cruell & feirce stormes, deangerous to travill to known places, much more to serch an unknown coast'.

The Pilgrims were also frightened of the wild beasts that might lie in wait: 'Besids, what could they see but a hidious & desolate wildernes, full of wild beasts & willd men? and what multituds ther might be of them they knew not. Nether could they, as it were, goe up to the tope of Pisgah, to vew from this willdernes a more goodly cuntrie to feed their hops: for which way soever they turnd their eys (save upward to the heavens) they could have little solace or content in respect of any outward objects. For summer being done, all things stand upon them with a weatherbeaten face; and the whole countrie, full of woods & thickets, represented a wild & savage heiw'.

Bradford knew, however, that there was no going back: 'If they looked behind them, ther was the mighty ocean which they had passed, and was now as a maine barr & goulfe to seperate them from all the civill parts of the world. If it be said they had a ship to sucour them, it is trew; but what heard they daly from the master & company? but that with speede they should looke out a place with their shallop, wher they would be at some near distance; for the season was shuch as he would not stirr from thence till a safe harbor was discovered by them wher they would be, and he might goe without danger; and that victells consumed apace, but he must & would keepe sufficient for them selves & their returne'.

And against this background, mutiny had now become a possibility among the disenchanted shipload — or at least desertion, as Captain Jones and his impatient *Mayflower* crew wanted to be gone. 'It was muttered by some, that if they gott not a place in time, they would turne them & their goods ashore & leave them. Let it also be considred what weake hopes of supply & succoure they left behinde them, that might bear up their minds in this sade condition and trialls they were under; and they could not but be very smale'.

Nor could Reverend John Robinson and their brother Pilgrims back in Leyden help them now. Bradford mused: 'It is true, indeed, the affections & love of their brethren at Leyden was cordiall & entire towards them, but they had litle power to help them, or them selves; and how the case stode between them & the marchants at their coming away, hath allready been declared. What could now sustaine them but the spirite of God & his grace? May not & ought not the children of these fathers rightly say: Our faithers were Englishmen which came over this great ocean, and were ready to perish in this willdernes'.

The Pilgrims held discussions and prayer sessions to give them the courage to go ashore and tackle the tasks of founding a settlement. To gain inspiration in their weakened state for this formidable task they cited precedents where, throughout history, others had wandered in the wilderness in a solitary way but had been unable to find a city to dwell in before hunger and thirst overcame them. This bolstered their spirits, especially as they believed God was behind their safe arrival. So they thanked Him for his goodness, and for his wonderful works to the children of men and decided to get on with the job. Bradford quoted prophetically Deuteronomy 26.5: 'and they sojourned there with a few, but became there a nation, great, mighty, and populous'.

The *Mayflower* was moored at the top of Cape Cod. It appeared to be a good spot for a settlement and was certainly large enough for the *Mayflower*. Winslow described how they came to an anchor in the Bay. He wrote it was good harbor and pleasant bay; circled round, except in the entrance, which is about four miles over from land to land; compassed about to the very sea, with oaks, pines, juniper, sassafras, and other sweet wood. He described it as a harbor wherein a thousand sail of ships may safely ride.

It was important that the Pilgrims start off their life in the new colony on the right foot and so the leaders decided to create an Agreement to be signed by everybody, which established the principles, rules and regulations of the new colony from the start. Bradford wrote that this Agreement was organized before people were allowed go ashore. Consequently there was 'a combination made' which was to serve as a foundation document 'being the first foundation of their governmente in this place'.

This Agreement was necessary, because not all the Pilgrims shared the same religious convictions. During the difficult voyage some of the less devout of the Pilgrim group had become dissatisfied, even to muttering rebellious sentiments. Bradford confirmed that this Agreement was 'occasioned partly by the discontented & mutinous speeches that some of the strangers amongst them had let fall from them in the ship'. Evidently these rebels, aware that the *Mayflower* had landed in the wrong spot had threatened 'That when they came a shore they would use their owne libertie; for none had power to command them, the patente they had being for Virginia, and not for New-england, which belonged to an other Government, with which the Virginia Company had nothing to doe'.

This Agreement came to be known as The Mayflower Compact. Bradford recorded: 'The forme was as followeth'.

'In the name of God, Amen. We whose names are underwritten, the loyall subjects of our dread soveraigne Lord, King James, by the grace

Early European images of the Indians idealized them, with biblical analogies to Adam and Eve.

of God, of Great Britaine, Franc, & Ireland king, defender of the faith, &c. haveing undertaken, for the glorie of God, and advancemente of the Christian faith, and honour of our king & countrie, a voyage to plant the first colonie in the Northerne parts of Virginia, doe by these presents solemnly & mutualy in the presence of God, and one of another, covenant & combine our selves togeather into a civill body politick, for our better ordering & preservation & furtherance of the ends aforesaid,; and by vertue herof to enacte, constitute, and frame such just & equall lawes, ordinances, acts, constitutions, & offices, from time to time, as shall be thought most meete & convenient for the generall good of the Colonie, unto which we promise all due submission and obedience. In witnes wherof we have herunder subscribed our names at Cap-Codd the 11 of November, in the year of the raigne of our soveraigne lord, King James, of England, France, & Ireland the eighteenth, and of Scotland the fiftie fourth. An°: Dom. 1620'.

The Mayflower Compact was agreed to by the majority of the Pilgrims, as forty-one of the sixty-five adult male passengers signed the document. However, there were some who were not party to the arrangement.

Having established this constitutional document for their new colony, the Pilgrims then selected a leader: 'They chose, or rather confirmed, Mr. John Carver (a man godly & well approved amongst them) their Governour for that year'.

At last they went ashore, landing at the tip of Cape Cod. The Pilgrims were on American soil for the first time. Winslow wrote that they supplied themselves with wood and water, and refreshed their people; while their shallop was fitted to coast the Bay to search for a habitation. It looked as if the Pilgrims would eat well; there was obviously a great store of fowl. Had they come prepared for it they could also have started a local whaling business; every day they saw whales playing hard by them. The Master and his Mate, and others experienced in fishing, professed they might have made £3,000 or £4,000 worth of oil. Impressively, they thought it better even than Greenland whale-fishing. The Pilgrims also found great mussels, very fat and full of sea pearl but perhaps having gorged themselves too enthusiastically they all found they 'could not eat them, for they made them all sick; the sailors as well as the passengers'.

Unfortunately at the tip of Cape Cod the bay was so shallow that the *Mayflower* had to be moored a long way out, forcing the Pilgrims to struggle ashore in the chill November temperatures. Winslow wrote that they could not come near the shore by three-quarters of an English mile; because of shallow water 'which was a great prejudice to them'. He said they 'were forced to wade a bow-shot or two, in going aland; which caused many to get colds and coughs: for it was, many times, freezing cold weather'.

After their initial excursion to shore in search of wood and water, a second landing party was then organized to get some more wood for the fire and search for Indians. As soon as they could, they sent ashore fifteen or sixteen men, well armed. This second landing party established that they were on the Cape Cod peninsula but they could not find any Indians.

They found it to be a small neck of land. On the one side, where they lay, was the Bay; and on the further side, the sea. The ground consisted of sandhills, described by Winslow as much like the downs of Holland, but much better ... 'The crust of the earth, at a spit's depth, is excellent black earth: all wooded with oaks, pines, sassafras, juniper, birch, holly, vines, some ash, walnut. The wood for the most part open, and without underwood; fit either to go, or ride, in'. Winslow reported that the second landing party did not find 'any person, nor habitation: and laded their boat with juniper, which smelled very sweet and strong; and of which they burnt, the most part of the time they lay there'.

12 November   On the second day the Pilgrims honored the Sabbath, organizing a special prayer service during which they gave thanks to God for delivering them across the seas of the vast Atlantic. Much of the rest of the day was spent discussing their various options. Some wanted to go ashore and build a settlement where they were, but others wanted to explore the Bay further in the shallop they had brought for this purpose. Most of the Pilgrims took the opportunity to rest and gather strength for the next day, while others collected their belongings together in preparation for going ashore. Captain Standish, as the military officer responsible for their safety, cleaned and checked their arsenal in anticipation of conflict with the Indians once they did go ashore.

13 November   By the third day, most of the Pilgrims believed that they could explore their new home best by boat. Bradford: 'and necessitie calling them to looke out a place for habitation, (as well as the maisters & mariners importunitie) they having brought a large shalop with them out of England, stowed in quarters in the ship, they now gott her out & sett their carpenters to work to trime her up; but being much brused & shatered in the shipe with foule weather, they saw she would be longe in mending'.

Nobody wanted to wait around while the boat was being repaired, especially as the rank and file in the Pilgrim group had been anxious to get ashore and wash their filthy clothes in the freshwater ponds near the tip of Cape Cod and so a third landing party was organized. Winslow wrote that their people went on shore to refresh themselves; and their women to wash. This domestic expedition constituted the third landing party.

14 November

On the fourth day, with the carpenter repairing the shallop and the women washing and drying the clothes which had been nine weeks in the confined hold below decks, the landing site was already a hive of activity.

Captain Standish, anxious not to waste a minute, prepared the arms and ammunition for an expedition on land, as by now most of the Pilgrim leaders agreed that they could not afford to wait until the boat was fixed before they found a spot to build their homes.

15 November

On the fifth day, the Pilgrims decided to venture out into the unknown and find out as much as they could about their new home. So a fourth landing party was organized, made up of armed men. It was a dangerous expedition but sixteen men volunteered without hesitation. And so, with cautious directions and instructions they set out — with every man carrying his musket, sword, and wearing his corslet — under the conduct of Captain Myles Standish. This well-armed expedition was looking for Indians, and searching for a river besides which they could establish their settlement.

Bradford continued the story: 'They sett forth the 15 of Novebr' in a single file and 'when they had marched aboute the space of a mile by the sea side, they espied 5 or 6 persons with a dogg coming towards them, who were salvages; but they fled from them, & ranne up into the woods, and the English followed them partly to see if they could speake with them, and partly to discover if ther might not be more of them lying in ambush. But the Indeans seeing them selves thus followed, they againe forsooke the woods, & rane away on the sands as hard as they could, so as they could not come near them, but followed them by the tracte of their feet sundrie miles'. Winslow estimated that they followed them for about ten miles, but then as darkness fell, they made their camp: 'So, night coming on, they made their randevous & set out their sentinels, and rested in quiete that night'.

16 November

Having spent their first night on dry land in America, not far from Stevens Point where they had landed the day before, the Pilgrims awoke on the sixth day and continued the chase. They had seen their first Indians and hoped to catch up with them. Their one worry was whether their supplies of food and drink held out. As Winslow said, they were ill-prepared because they had taken neither beer, nor water with them and the only supplies they had were biscuit and Holland cheese, and a little bottle of aqua vitae.

Nevertheless, they followed the Indians to East Harbor Creek and then through a part of Truro, called East Harbor, before getting lost 'and the next morning followed their tracte till they had headed a great creake, & so left the sands, & turned an other way into the woods. But they still followed them by geuss, hopeing to find their dwellings; but they soone lost both them & them selves, falling into shuch thickets as were ready to tear their cloaths & armore in peeces, but were most distresed for wante of drinke'. Here at Dyers Water Hole the Pilgrims saw a deer and tasted the sparkling New England water: 'at length they found water & refreshed them selves, being the first New-England water they drunke of, and was now in thir great thirste as pleasante unto them as wine or bear had been in for-times'.

Near one of the waterholes, they then stumbled across an old Indian campsite. Here were some Indian graves full of artefacts, most of which they put back out of respect for the dead: 'Afterwards they directed their course to come to the other shore, for they knew it was a necke of land they were to crosse over, and so at length gott to the sea-side, and marched to this supposed river, & by the way found a pond of clear fresh water, and shortly after a good quantitie of clear ground wher the Indeans had formerly set corne, and some of their graves'.

Next the expedition found evidence of an even more substantial settlement left behind by a shipwrecked sailor of long ago as Bradford recounted: 'And proceeding furder they saw new-stuble wher corne had been set the same year', also they found wher latly a house had been, wher some planks and a great ketle was remaining'. Winslow says this had been a ship's kettle, which had been brought out of Europe. They also found many walnut trees, full of nuts; and great store of strawberries; and some vines.

But then, more importantly, they came across their first food supplies. Bradford related how they saw 'heaps of sand newly padled' which 'they, digging up, found in them diverce faire Indean baskets filled with corne, and some in eares, faire and good, of diverce collours, which seemed to them a very goodly sight, (haveing never seen any shuch before)'. Winslow tells us there were some thirty six ears of corn, some yellow, and some red, and others mixed with blue. The basket was round, and narrow at the top. It held about three or four bushels; which was as much as two of them could lift up from the ground, and was beautifully made.

The Pilgrims did not know whether to keep the European kettle and the corn. Winslow described how they were in suspense about what to do with these. At length they concluded to take the kettle, and as much of the corn as they could carry away with them. They did not consider that they were stealing, in fact; they would return the kettle as soon as the Indians asked for it back and when they were able they would give the Indians the same amount of corn from their own supplies.

So the Pilgrims loaded themselves up with this God-sent food supply. Winslow said they took all the ears and some of the loose corn in the kettle, which two men carried away on a staff. Others filled their pockets and what they could not take away they buried because they were so laden with armor, that they could not carry all the corn.

Bradford believed they had found the Pamet River where they might have been able to establish their settlement, as 'This was near the place of that supposed river they came to seeck'. Bradford also noted that the Pamet River branched into a second stream, the Little Pamet River or Hopkins Creek, overlooked by Tom's Bluff and that there were empty canoes on the banks on each side of the river indicating that Indians crossed at this point. This river 'unto which they wente and found it to open it selfe into 2 armes with a high cliffe of sand in the enterance, but more like to be crikes of salte water then any fresh, for ought they saw; and that ther was good harborige for their shalope; leaving it further to be discovered by their shalop when she was ready'.

The expedition had been commanded to be away for no more than two days so they pitched a final camp that night at a freshwater pond making a great fire and building a barricade. Three sentries kept watch throughout the night during which it hardly stopped raining.

17 November   The Pilgrims had now been in the colony a week.

Confused and weak, the members of the fourth expedition now lost their way as they tried to return to the ship. While they were lost Bradford stepped into an Indian tree sapling trap. Winslow said that they came to a tree where a young sapling was bent over to form a trap with some acorns strewed about. Although some of them understood what it was and Stephen Hopkins said that it had been set to catch some deer, others were less wary and as they were looking at it, William Bradford came up the rear and walked right into it. The sapling gave a sudden jerk upwards and Bradford was immedately pulled up into the air by the leg. Despite Bradford's distress, Winslow was impressed with the trap and claimed that it was as well made as any English model he had ever seen.

Once they cut the sorry Bradford down the Pilgrims continued looking for their way back to the ship. This was not easy and by the time they got out of the wood they were a mile too high above the creek. There they saw three bucks, some partridges and, as they came along by a creek, they noticed great flocks of wild geese and ducks. Winslow said the birds were very fearful of them.

By now out of food and water, the Pilgrim party was desperate to reach the *Mayflower*. So they marched some through the woods, along the sands, and waded through the water up to their knees, till, at length, they sighted the ship. Relieved to spot their companions, the land expedition then signalled to be rescued and the long boat came to fetch them. Winslow said that Master Jones and Master Carver, being on shore at the time also came to meet them.

So their first major expedition inland was a great success. They had seen their first Indians; gained some idea of the Indian camps and explored other settlements in the area; discovered how the Indians buried their dead and hid their corn; and had brought some of the latter back to the settlement as the first real produce of the land. Winslow said that they then delivered the corn into the store, to be kept for seed because they did not know how long it would be before they would sight any more. The relief was felt by all. Bradford said: 'And so like the men from Eshcoll they carried with them the fruits of the land, & showed their breethren; of which, & their returne, they were marvelusly glad, and their harts incouraged'.

18 November   On the eighth day in the colony the explorers took a rest. With the help of their fellow Pilgrims the sixteen members of the inland expedition now changed their clothes, cleaned their arms and ammunition, enjoyed some square meals and rested up so that they could return to the East Creek area and continue their search for the Indians.

Although some of the Pilgrims wanted to mount another expedition on land, the general opinion was to wait until the little shallop was ready, so they could explore more effectively. Some of the group were impatient to get off the ship and onto dry land so they could establish their settlement, especially as Captain Jones and the *Mayflower* could not stay in New England forever. They had to get off the ship sooner or later.

19 November   On the ninth day the Pilgrims commemorated the Sabbath with their usual service on board. Special prayers of thanksgiving were said, acknowledging the safe return of Captain Standish, William Bradford and the sixteen-man expedition which had been away in the wilderness for three days.

20 November   Their tenth day in the colony marked the start of a waiting period. Winslow said that although the members of the land exploration were keen to set out again, and had hoped their shallop would be ready in five or six days, at the longest, their carpenter was repairing the little boat very slowly.

For the next week the Pilgrims were forced to amuse themselves around the ship and immediate bay area while the carpenter did his best.

27 November   At last, on the seventeenth day in the colony, the shallop was ready for its maiden voyage down south towards East Harbor's Pamet River. Bradford said that even Captain Jones accompanied the thirty-four man party of Pilgrims and *Mayflower* crew: 'the shalop being got ready, they set out againe for the better discovery of this place, & the master of the ship desired to goe him selfe, so ther went some 30 men but found it to be no harbor for ships but only for boats'. Winslow said they made Captain Jones their leader for this expedition as a compliment, in order to thank him for his kindness.

Due to the number of men involved in this expedition, they decided to take both the shallop and the long boat. The going was not easy however and before long some of them had to get out of the boat and walk in the freezing water. Winslow said that soon after they set forth the weather became rough and they were met by cross winds, so they had to drag the boat into the nearest beach.

Conditions then became so bad that they decided to abandon the boats at Beach Point and continue on foot. Winslow said they then marched six or seven miles further, having left some of the party in the boats in the hope that they could sail after them when conditions changed.

28 November   Next day Winslow said some of the party reached the foot of Old Tom's Hill, which lay between the two creeks. They then marched some four or five miles by the Pamet River itself, the larger of the two creeks, and the shallop followed them.

Then, despite the fact that most of the party wanted to keep exploring the Pamet River bank, Captain Jones declared he was exhausted and demanded that they stop and camp for the night. This was a fortunate decision as they were able to shoot some game over-night. Winslow said the men had become tired of marching up and down the steep hills and deep valleys, which lay half a foot thick with snow, and so they camped the night under a few pine trees. Having shot three fat geese and six ducks they had a good supper, which he said they ate with soldiers' stomachs, for they had eaten little that day. Next day, they planned to go up to the head of the river to find fresh water.

29 November   After another cold night, the Pilgrims woke up on their nineteenth day ashore.

Their plans to follow the larger Pamet River were abandoned however in favor of searching for more corn. Winslow related how they did not like the hilliness of the soil or the bad conditions in the harbor. So they turned towards another creek, hoping to go over and look for the rest of the corn that they left behind when they were there before.

As they marched north from the river to Corn Hill, they were lucky enough to stumble across a canoe which enabled them to bag some game for lunch. Winslow said that, when they came to the creek, they saw the canoe beached on dry ground near a flock of geese in the river, at which one of them made a shot, and killed a couple of them. They then launched the canoe and fetched the geese and then crossed the creek seven or eight at a time.

Then, in search of more easy food, they managed to find their way back to the place where they had found the corn earlier, which they now named Cornhill. After digging around for a while they then found the rest of the corn. They were very happy.

While they were digging about in this buried Indian food larder, they uncovered some other valuable items including a bottle of oil and two or three baskets full of Indian wheat, a bag of beans, with a good many wheat ears, and more corn, which Winslow said was in all about ten bushels. This would serve them well for seed.

Because the Pilgrims had arrived in America so late in the year they would probably have starved to death if they had not found all this Indian corn. Winslow described how the ground was now covered with snow and so frozen that they were barely able, with their cutlasses and short swords, to cut into the ground a foot deep. Unfortunately, Winslow said, they had forgotten to bring any other tools. Nevertheless Bradford noted: 'And here is to be noted a spetiall providence of God, and a great mercie to this poore people, that hear they gott seed to plant them corne the next year, or els they might have starved, for they had none, nor any liklyhood to get any till the season had beene past. Neither is it lickly they had had this, if the first viage had not been made, for the ground was now all covered with snow, & hard frozen'.

Storms then threatened to interrupt the collection of the corn; Captain Jones insisted on going back to look after his ship. Not everyone wanted to go, however; according to Winslow some of them wanted to stay and explore the Indians' habitations. So they sent home their weakest people and all the corn, while eighteen of the others stayed and camped there that night. They wanted the shallop to return to them next day, and bring back some mattocks and spades.

Meanwhile, back on the *Mayflower*, the first American Pilgrim was born in the colony. Recording the birth Winslow said it pleased God that Mistress White was brought to bed of a son which was called Peregrine.

30 November   The Pilgrims had now been in the colony for twenty days.

After another cold night, the members of the fifth expedition woke determined to find an Indian village. Winslow described how they then followed certain beaten paths of the Indians into the woods in the hope that these would lead them to some town or houses. After walking for a while, they hit upon a very broad beaten path, two feet wide. Thinking they were about to confront Indians they got their guns ready but it was a false alarm. The path did not lead to a household but to an animal stockade. Winslow said that they then prepared their guns for shooting because they concluded they were near the Indian dwellings but, in the end, they found it to be only a path designed to drive along deer into a hunting trap.

The Pilgrim party continued to pursue the Indians. Although they could not find any living Indians, they did find some corpses in this spot. They began to realize it was a graveyard of sorts. Winslow said that when they had marched five or six miles into the woods, and could find no signs of any people, they returned again another way. And as they came into cleared ground, they found a place like a grave except that it was much bigger and longer than any they had yet seen. It was also covered with boards which puzzled them, so they resolved to dig it up.

A description of the things found inside the tomb is provided by Winslow; they found first a mat, and under that a beautiful bow and

The early explorers were fascinated by the Indians and took great pains to record their clothing, weapons and domestic utensils.

then another mat and under that, a board finely carved and painted, with three broaches on the top like a crown.

The investigators dug deeper and, between the mats, they found bowls, trays, dishes, and such like trinkets. At length, they came to a beautiful new mat and, under that, two bundles — a large and a small one. They opened the largest bundle to find a great quantity of fine and red powder and the bones and skull of a man. The skull still had fine yellow hair on it and a little flesh. In with the skull there were also a knife, a pack-needle, and two or three old iron implements. The whole package was bound up in a sailor's canvas cassock, and a pair of cloth breeches. Winslow said the red powder was a kind of embalming liquid and yielded a strong, but not offensive, smell.

Then, lifting the smaller corpse out of the grave, the Pilgrims removed some of the trinkets. They opened the smaller bundle finding the same powder in it, and the bones and head of a little child. The legs and other parts were bound with strings and bracelets of fine white beads. There was also alongside the baby corpse a little bow, about three-quarters long and some other odd items. Winslow said the Pilgrims took some of the prettiest things away with them and covered up the corpse again.

Winslow related how no one knew the identity of the yellow-haired corpse but there was variety of opinions among them about this embalmed person. Some thought it was an Indian lord and King, while others argued that, as the Indians all have black hair and none had ever been seen with brown or yellow hair, the corpse could have been a Christian of special note, who had died among the Indians and who had been buried in honor. Others thought the Indians had killed him and buried him in this style to triumph over him.

Then, at last loaded up with their spoils from the grave, the Pilgrims heard about some nearby Indian shelters which turned out to be much more substantial structures than they had imagined and full of many more attractive goods. While they were searching the graves, two of the sailors who had come on shore by chance, found two houses full of goods but empty for the moment. The sailors, having their guns and hearing nobody, entered the houses and took away some things before coming and telling Winslow's expedition party. Seven or eight of the expedition party went with the sailors to inspect the homes.

Winslow described how the Indian houses were made with young sapling trees, bent over with both ends stuck in the ground. They were shaped round like an arbor, he said, and covered down to the ground with thick and well wrought mats while the door was not over a yard high, made of a mat which opened and shut. The chimney was a wide open hole in the top with a mat which they could use to cover it whenever they pleased. The huts were tall enough for the Pilgrims to stand and go upright in them. In the midst of them were four small trenches cut into the ground; small sticks were laid over the trenches and, on these, they hung their pots. The Indians lay around the fire on mats which served as their beds. The houses were double-matted being matted without and also within, with newer and 'fairer' mats.

As for the furniture and fittings, they found wooden bowls, trays, and dishes; earthen pots; hand baskets made of crab shells and also an English pail or bucket which lacked a bail, but had two iron ears. There were also baskets of different sorts curiously made with black and white threads. The Pilgrims also found two or three deers' heads — one which had been recently killed, for it was still fresh.

Winslow said they also saw 'a company' of deer's feet stuck up in the houses along with horns and eagles' claws. There were also two or three baskets full of parched acorns, pieces of fish, and a piece of a broiled herring. They found also a little silk grass, and a little tobacco seed with some other seeds which they could not recognize.

Although they could have expected to find some more food, they could only find some rotting meat. A disappointed Winslow said they found inside a hollow tree, two or three pieces of venison but thought it fitter for the dogs than for them. Nevertheless rather than return empty-handed, the Pilgrims decided to take the most valuable items from the Indian homes. Winslow confessed that they took away some of the best things with them but left the houses standing as they were.

As darkness fell the Pilgrims hurried back to the ship. Winslow announced that they had planned to leave some beads and other things in the houses as a sign of peace and that they meant to trade with the Indians but they had no time. However as soon as they could meet up with the Indians they would give them full satisfaction.

1 December The Pilgrims, all now back on the ship, had been in the colony for three weeks. The exploring party showed all the goods that they had taken from the graves and the houses to the other Pilgrims. By now they were beginning to have some understanding of their environment through some idea of the local rivers and the settlement patterns of the Indians but as yet they still had not selected a site for the settlement.

4 December Edward Thompson, the servant to William White, became the first Pilgrim to die in Cape Cod Harbor. A party took him ashore and dug a grave at Long Point, which was the start of a sad little graveyard. Even though new Pilgrims had been born, with his death, their numbers still stood at 102.

5 December On this their twenty-fifth day in the colony, the Pilgrims nearly lost another person through the foolishness of a boy who was playing with gunpowder.

Winslow related that Francis Billington, the son of John Billington, escaped a great danger in his father's absence when he found some gunpowder and a fowling piece charged and had shot the gun off in his father's cabin.

A small fire broke out as a result. The cabin almost caught fire, and came within four feet of the bed between the decks. It was a lucky escape because if the ship had burnt down the Pilgrims would have lost their only home. However by God's mercy, no harm was done, Winslow said.

6 December   The *Mayflower* had been moored at the tip of Cape Cod for twenty-six days and still everybody was crowded on board. By now most people thought it was about time that they selected a place to build their village. More than 100 people remained pressed below decks in the most cramped and uncomfortable quarters. Wading through the cold water and living in damp clothes had given many of the Pilgrims colds and in the confined quarters chest infections spread throughout the group.

Despite all this, they could not yet agree where to live. It was like the problem of deciding whether to go to Guiana or Virginia all over again. The group was so democratic that everyone had to have their say and all opinions had to be carefully weighed.

The pro-Cape Cod lobby group claimed they should get off the ship where they were and start a settlement near the Pamet River at the north end of the Cape Cod peninsula. This Pamet River group claimed that it was a convenient harbor for boats; the soil was obviously good for growing corn as the buried corn demonstrated; the fishing and whaling were excellent; it was a healthy and secure location that could be easily defended; and now that it was too cold to go out searching for a better spot it was important to get ashore and build warm shelters before everyone died from the cold or related diseases.

As it was, even now, they claimed the cold and wet lodgings had affected them all with vehement coughs; their lives were already in danger because the *Mayflower* had become a contaminated and sickly ship breeding infection and disease. Finally, the food was running out fast and before long they would not even have meat, butter or beer to give them the energy they needed to build their homes. Once the food stocks began to disappear the *Mayflower* would have to take off and return to England, leaving them to fend for themselves.

But the anti-Cape Cod group wanted to go north to Ipswich which they believed would have a better harbor, better soil and better fishing. This group said it would be foolish to settle down without looking around more, and that there was no fresh running water locally, only ponds.

After a long discussion the Pilgrims compromised and decided to look for a better spot than the Pamet River, but within the greater Cape Cod Harbor itself. In consequence, the *Mayflower's* pilot Richard Coppin suggested they go and look at the river which flowed out into the bay at Plymouth Harbor, across the bay from where they were now.

A ten-man party set out on what was to be a seven-day trip (their

Contemporary rendition of an Indian warrior.

sixth land expedition since arriving). This time they headed south alongside the Cape Cod peninsula opposite Truro, aiming for Bilingsgate Point. Winslow described how the party was led by Captain Standish, and included William Bradford as official recorder, Master Carver, himself (also keeping notes), John Tilley, Edward Tilley, John Howland, Richard Warren, Stephen Hopkins and Edward Doty. There were also two seamen, John Allerton and Thomas English. Two of the Master's Mates, from the *Mayflower* also went — Master Clarke and Master Coppin — along with the Master Gunner, and three sailors.

Unfortunately for this party the extreme cold almost immobilized some of them, including the Tilley brothers, who 'swooned', while the Master Gunner was also very sick. Bradford said: 'The weather was very could, & it frose so hard as the sprea of the sea lighting on their coats, they were as if they had been glased'.

Despite the icy temperatures, they reached Billingsgate Point and then sailed into Wellfleet Harbor circling around and heading south abreast of the western beaches of Eastham. Here, they landed north of the Great Pond. Just before dark they spotted some Indians, as Bradford reported: 'that night betimes they gott downe into the botome of the bay, and as they drue nere the shore they saw some 10 or 12 Indeans very busie about some thing. They landed about a league or 2 from them, and had much a doe to put a shore any wher, it lay so full of flats. Being landed, it grew late, and they made them selves a barricade with loggs & bowes as well as they could in the time, & set out their sentenill & betooke them to rest, and saw the smoake of the fire the savages made that night'.

Meanwhile, back on the *Mayflower*, Jasper More, a servant of Governor Carver's, died. His body was taken ashore to buried.

Now there were only 101 Pilgrims left.

7 December   Having survived the night, Bradford recounted how they woke on the twenty-seventh day determined to find a spot to build their village and expecting to meet the Indians they had seen from the boat the night before. The team split up, with some going around the Wellfleet Harbor area in the boat and others on foot. 'When morning was come they devided their company, some to coaste along the shore in the boate, and the rest marched throw the woods to see the land, if any fit place might be for their dwelling'.

Bradford went on to say how they found it difficult to locate the Indians even though they followed them to the Great Pond area of Eastham. Winslow also agreed that they followed the tracks of the Indian's 'bare feet' a good way on the sands until they at length saw where the Indians struck into the woods, by the side of a pond. Then, as they went to view the place, one of the Pilgrims said he thought he saw an Indian house among the trees. So they went to investigate but did not find any Indian homes, although they ventured a long way into the woods.

Indeed, they seemed destined to find dead Indians rather than live ones. Once again they came across an Indian graveyard. Winslow said that they found a great burying place which was surrounded with a large wall like a churchyard, with young posts, four or five yards long, set as close to each other as they could be. Inside the fence it was full of graves, big and small. Some graves were fenced themselves and others had an Indian house made over them, although not matted. These were more sumptuous than the graves at Cornhill. This time they did not dig any of them up but only viewed them, and went away.

Then at last they established that they were indeed in the land of the living when they found some new Indian homes and possessions in this Eastham area. Winslow said that as they explored they found four or five Indian houses, which had been inhabited but were uncovered, and had no mats in them. There was nothing left inside but for two or three pieces of old mat. A little further on, they found two baskets full of parched acorns hidden in the ground which they supposed had been corn.

As the sun set, the explorers managed to return to the beach near Eastham's Great Meadow Creek and the safety of their boat, which was a relief to them all. Bradford: 'When the sune grue low, they hasted out of the woods to meete with their shallop, to whom they made signes to come to them into a creeke hardby, the which they did at highwater; of which they were very glad, for they had not seen each other all that day, since the morning'.

Not wishing to take any risks that night they built a temporary fort in the Eastham area. Bradford pointed out it was just as well they did: 'So they made them a barricado (as usually they did every night) with loggs, staks, & thike pine bowes, the height of a man, leaving it open to leeward, partly to shelter them from the could & wind (making their fire in the midle, & lying rounde aboute it), and partly to defend them from any sudden assaults of the savags, if they should surround them. So being very weary, they betooke them to rest'. Winslow said that they took the usual precaution of setting a watch.

So far so good, but then in the middle of the night they had to leap to their feet and fire off a couple of shots in response to a false alarm. Bradford: 'Aboute midnight, they heard a hideous & great crie, and their sentinell caled, "Arme, arme"; so they bestired them & stood to their armes, & shote of a cupple of moskets, and then the noys seased. They concluded it was a companie of wolves, or such like willd beasts; for one of the sea men tould them he had often heard shuch a noyse in New-found land'.

While Bradford was away on this trip, his wife Dorothy fell overboard and drowned in the icy waters of Cape Cod Harbor. Now there were only 100 Pilgrims left. Although Bradford must have been devastated by this tragic accident, he did not record it in his journal.

8 December   The Pilgrims had been in the colony one month. Aware that time was slipping away from them, the expedition rose determined to find a spot for a settlement. In fact, Bradford maintained they only 'rested till about 5 of the clock in the morning; for the tide, & ther purpose to goe from thence, made them be stiring betimes'. Winslow said that two or three, who doubted whether their pieces would fire off or not, tested them out to be safe.

Before leaving the Eastham camp site they gave thanks for their deliverance from the terrors of the night. They intended to set off in search of the elusive settlement site, this time heading west along the increasingly wide stem of the Cape Cod peninsula towards Plymouth itself. 'So after praier they prepared for breakfast, and it being day dawning, it was thought best to be carring things downe to the boate.'

They debated whether to put their arms straight into the boat, or whether to keep them for protection while they were decamping. Some complained their guns were heavy and they were sick of carrying them but others said they would be killed if the Indians suddenly appeared and caught them unarmed. In the end, most of them made the mistake of deciding to leave their guns on the beach. 'As it fell out, the water being not high enough, they layed them down on the banke side, & came up to breakfast.'

It was at this worst possible moment that they were caught out. Bradford: 'presently, all on the sudain, they heard a great & strange crie, which they knew to be the same voyces they heard in the night, though they varied their notes, & one of their company being abroad came runing in, & cried, "Men, Indeans, Indeans"; and withall, their arowes came flying amongst them'.

This certainly was not how the Pilgrims had planned to begin their relationship with the Indians, yet they had no alternative but to grab their guns and fight. It was twenty Pilgrims and friends against forty Indians — with the latter fit and well and on their home ground.

Bradford described this important battle: 'Their men rane with all speed to recover their armes, as by the good providence of God they did. In the mean time, of those that were ther ready, two muskets were discharged at them, & 2 more stood ready in the enterance of ther randevoue, but were comanded not to shoote till they could take full aime at them; & the other 2 charged againe with all speed, for ther were only 4 had armes ther, & defended the baricado which was first assalted'.

Naturally the Pilgrims did not want to leave this fort, in case the Indians shot them when they were out in the open or took the fort once they left it. As Winslow said, they thought it best to defend their position in case the enemy overpowered them and took their possessions and in future had a greater advantage against them.

At the same time they were also concerned not to lose the boat and hoped that the other sixteen Pilgrims would be able to defend it. Winslow said their care was no less for the shallop but they hoped all the others would defend the boat. Those in the fort called out to those in the boat to make sure they were surviving. They answered 'Well! Well!', he claimed and so instructed Winslow and his party in the fort to 'Be of good courage!'.

Winslow said they then heard three of the guns of the people in the boat being fired off. Then those guarding the boat called for help in lighting their guns and for a firebrand to light their matches, so without hesitation one of the Pilgrims from the fort took a log out of the fire on his shoulder and carried it to the boat. This, Winslow said, impressed the Indians greatly.

Bradford continued: 'The crie of the Indeans was dreadfull, espetially when they saw ther men rune out of the randevoue towourds the shallop, to recover their armes, the Indeans wheeling aboute upon them'. Winslow described how the cries of Indians sounded like 'Woath! Woach Ha! Ha! Hach! Woach!'.

Nevertheless, with their superior weapons, the Pilgrims soon gained the upper hand. Those who had dashed down the beach to grab their guns from where they left them on the sand then turned them against the Indians: 'some running out with coats of malle on, & cutlasses in their hands, they soone got their armes, & let flye amongs them, and quickly stopped their violence'.

So the Pilgrims forced back the forty Indians and won the first round against their reluctant American hosts. Fortunately, they had done so without injuries, too. Despite the victory, however, the Pilgrims much admired the courage of their aggressors, particularly one heroic Indian, who was thought to be their leader. Bradford described him as 'a lustie man, and no less valiante', who 'stood behind a tree within halfe a musket shot, and let his arrows flie at them. He was seen shoot 3 arrowes, which were all avoyded. He stood 3 shot of a musket, till one taking full aime at him, and made the barke or splinters of the tree fly about his ears, after which he gave an extraordinary shrike, and away they wente all of them'.

After the Indians had been repelled, some of the braver Pilgrims ran after them so as to demonstrate that they were not afraid: 'They left some to keep the shalop, and followed them aboute a quarter of a mille, and shouted once or twise, and shot of 2 or 3 peces, & so returned. This they did, that they might conceive that they were not affrade of them or any way discouraged'.

As a special memento of this encounter, Bradford related how they 'gathered up a bundle of their arrows, & sente them into England afterward by the master of the ship'. Winslow also wrote that some of these eighteen arrows were headed with brass, others were headed with animal horn and others were tipped with eagles' claws. He said that many more arrows were shot than those that were found. The Pilgrims decided to call this place, which was right in the middle of the Eastham area, 'the place of the first encounter'.

The Pilgrims did not think they were especially lucky to survive as they believed God had given them special deliverance from the arrows. They claimed it was symbolic that, although their coats left hanging in the trees were riddled with arrow holes, they themselves went unharmed. Bradford said they had escaped 'by his spetiall providence' and that God had protected them ensuring that 'not any one of them were either hurte, or hitt, though their arrows came close by them, & on every side them, and sundry of their coats, which hunge up in the barricado, were shot throw & throw'.

The party might have survived their first fight with the Indians but, even so, they were still no closer to finding a spot on shore to build their homes. They had been in the colony a month, an increasing number of people were sick and dying back on the crowded and infected *Mayflower* and yet the men still dithered about looking for the ideal settlement spot. On the return of this latest land expedition, in fact, the explorers heard that a fourth person had died, James Chilton, who was the head of a family household.

His death reduced the Pilgrim numbers to ninety-nine. If they did not move on shore and into warm shelter soon their numbers would be seriously reduced and they would lack the labor to carve a settlement out of the wilderness. Finding a settlement spot suddenly became a matter of extreme urgency.

7 Winter of Death

December 1620—March 1621

*But that which was most sadd &
lamentable was that in 2 or 3 moneths
time half of their company dyed,
espetialy in Jan. & February, being the
depth of winter, and wanting houses &
other comforts, being infected with the
scurvie & other diseases, which this long
vioage & their inacomodate condition
had brought upon them.*

William Bradford

**8 December
1620**

Following their close call with the Indians the Pilgrims decided to move
fast. They pushed off in their boat from Eastham into the bay and sailed
towards Plymouth to put as much distance as they could between them
and the Indians. Perhaps they could find a spot for a settlement further
west along the shore.

But this time luck was running against them, for they nearly drowned
as their boat began to break up when she sailed into violent surf. Their
pilot, Robert Coppin, had lost his way as Bradford reported: 'From
hence they departed, & costed all along, but discerned no place likly for
harbor; & therfore hasted to a place that their pillote, (one Mr. Coppin
who had bine in the cuntrie before) did assure them was a good harbor,
which he had been in, and they might fetch it before night; of which
they were glad, for it begane to be foule weather. After some houres
sailing, it begane to snow & raine, & about the middle of the afternoone,
the wind increased, & the sea became very rough, and they broake their
rudder, & it was as much as 2 men could doe to steere her with a
cupple of oares. But their pillott bade them be of good cheere, for he
saw the harbor'.

Then conditions deteriorated even further. They were blown off
course towards Duxbury Bay where they got caught up in the surf
between Gurnet Head and Saquish Point on the seaside of the entrance
to Duxbury Bay. Bradford: 'but the storme increasing, & night drawing
on, they bore what saile they could to gett in, while they could see. But
herwith they broake their mast in 3 peeces, & their saill fell over bord,
in a very grown sea, so as they had like to have been cast away'.

84

Their prospects looked grim in these conditions. All of them could have drowned if the boat had tipped over then, but, just as darkness fell, a fresh current swept the boat with its confused pilot west around Saquish Point, right into the peaceful waters of Duxbury Bay and onto the beach of Clark's island. Bradford: 'they recovered them selves, & having the floud with them, struck into the harbore. But when it came too, the pillott was deceived in the place, and he said his eys never saw that place before; & he & the master mate would have rune her ashore, in a cove full of breakers, before the winde'.

The pilot's confusion might have caused panic had not the day been saved when 'a lusty seaman which steered, bade those which rowed, that if they were men', they must turn the boat around fast 'or ells they were all cast away; the which they did with speed. So he bid them be of good cheere & row lustly, for ther was a faire sound before them, & he doubted not but they should find one place or other wher they might ride in saftie'.

This 'lusty seaman' was correct. After the crew had rowed the boat away from the beach and certain disaster 'and though it was very darke, and rained sore, yet in the end they gott under the lee of a smalle iland, and remained ther all that night in saftie'.

Having reached the island the Pilgrims would have loved to have collapsed in a huddle and gone to sleep but, having escaped dangerous Indians earlier that day, they were afraid to leave their boat for the shore. Bradford continued: 'they knew not this to be an iland till morning, but were devided in their minds; some would keepe the boate for fear they might be amongst the Indians'. In the end however some of the more daring clambered out of the boat and went into the trees and lit a fire because they were so weake and could, they could not endure, but got a shore, & with much adoe got fire, (all things being so wett) and the rest were glad to come to them; for after midnight the wind shifted to the north-west, & it frose hard'. Winslow also said they kept watch all night, even though it was raining.

9 December Waking up early because of the extreme cold, Winslow wrote that in the morning, they marched about and discovered that they were on an island. Fortunately they found no inhabitants on it. And here they decided to stay all that day, Saturday. Bradford wrote it 'was a faire sunshining day, and they found them sellvs to be on an island secure from the Indeans, wher they might drie their stufe, fixe their peeces, & rest them selves, and gave God thanks for his mercies, in their manifould deliverances'.

During the same day, back at the *Mayflower*, Chilton was buried in the little graveyard on shore.

10 December The exhausted and freezing Pilgrims kept the Sabbath by spending much of the day reading prayers and thanking God for their deliverance from the Indians and the storm. Bradford: 'and this being the last day of the weeke, they prepared ther to keepe the Sabath'. Apart from this they tried to dry off, keep warm by the fire and discussed where else they could look for a settlement site.

Sadly, four more people then died back at the ship — three from disease and a fourth by drowning. This brought the Pilgrim population down to ninety-five.

11 December
Forefathers'
Day

Starting out early in their boat the exploring party headed west across Duxbury Bay towards Plymouth where fortunately Bradford recounted that 'they sounded the harbor, and founde it fitt for shipping' which meant that *Mayflower* and other ships could get into this part of the bay.

Encouraged by this good deep water close to the shore they decided to disembark and see if the soil was suitable for a settlement. Although they may have been quite unaware of this historic moment, they then beached the boat at Plymouth Rock 'and marched into the land' at the very spot where they would subsequently establish Plymouth itself. Their hopes rose as they found all the right conditions for a settlement site, including 'diverse cornfeilds, & litle runing brooks' which made them decide, according to Bradford, that this was 'a place (as they supposed) fitt for situation; at least it was the best they could find, and the reason, & their presente necessitie, made them glad to accepte of it'.

12 December

Most of the Pilgrims agreed that this was the best spot they had seen in the month or so they had been searching around Cape Cod Bay. Bradford described how they clambered back into their boat and 'returned to their shipp againe with this news to the rest of their people, which did much comforte their harts'.

13 December

Captain Standish, William Bradford and other Pilgrims from the exploring party spent the day convincing members of the anti-Cape Cod group that Plymouth would be the best spot for a village, while others began to pack up their belongings in anticipation of the move ashore.

They decided to leave the ship where she was and sail and row the twenty-five miles west across Cape Cod Harbor to Plymouth in the open boat.

14 December

The first landing party was selected and this group then made the final preparations for the journey across the bay to their new home.

15 December

Although the Pilgrims had finally chosen the spot to build their village the weather conditions continued to frustrate them. Bradford: 'they wayed anchor to goe to the place they had discovered, & came within 2 leagues of it, but were faine to bear up again'. So they had to turn back and try again the next day.

16 December

Beaver and bear were welcome signs to Pilgrims searching for a bountiful spot to settle.

After nearly five weeks in the colony, the Pilgrims were finally going to be able to get off the *Mayflower* and make a start on shore. Bradford reported that 'the winde came faire, and they arrived safe in this harbor'. Even then they were lucky, however, as Winslow tells us, because conditions quickly changed; had they been any later they would have been driven back to the *Mayflower* once more.

The members of this initial settling party were excited to see the chosen spot at last; as they arrived, according to Bradford, they all 'tooke better view of the place, and resolved wher to pitch their dwelling'. They were overjoyed with their new location, Winslow explained, because the harbor was surrounded with good land and in the bay there were two fine islands which were uninhabited and on which there was a wide variety of trees including oak, pine, walnut, beech and sassafras.

In addition the Pilgrims, who were efficient hunters, imagined they would eat quite well. Winslow said there was a great store of fowl and predicted the bay would be full of different fish in the different seasons including skate, cod, turbot, and herring. He claimed there was also an abundance of mussels, crabs and lobsters. In all it was something of a Garden of Eden.

17 December

The Pilgrims observed the Sabbath and prayed for guidance for their transfer from the *Mayflower* to the shore and for the overwhelming task of building a village from scratch in the middle of this bitterly cold North American winter.

18 December

The moment had come at last. According to Winslow, they went ashore, with the Master of the ship, and three or four of the sailors. In order to find out the best place to start building the houses and see if there were any threatening Indians about they then marched along the coast towards Kingston, into the woods for some seven or eight miles. But they did not see any Indians or houses. However they did discover four or five small running brooks of very sweet fresh water.

It appeared the Pilgrim's luck had changed for the better. Not only did this spot have good fishing and fresh water, but Winslow said the land was an excellent black mould and there were many species of timber as well including oak, pine, walnut, beech, ash, birch, bazle, holly, sassafras, cherry-trees, plum-trees and many others which they could not identify. They also found many kinds of herbs, strawberry leaves, sorrel, yarrow, carvell, brook-lime, liverwort, watercresses, great store of leeks and onions and an excellent strong kind of flax and hemp. The area also contained useful sand gravel, excellent clay for pots, a great store of stone, though somewhat soft, and the best water that 'ever they drank'.

By now the explorers had found out enough to understand the shape of Cape Cod Bay. The wide expanse of water between them and the

Mayflower at the tip of Cape Cod appeared to Winslow to be shaped in fashion like a sickle or fish-hook.

The Pilgrims decided not to risk staying ashore without any shelters that night, so, many being weary with marching, they went on board again.

19 December

The next morning, Winslow wrote, they continued to look for the exact spot to settle. Some went on land, and some in the shallop. They found a creek, and went up three miles towards Kingston, finding the Jones's River which they described as a very pleasant river if a little shallow. Although at high tide a bark of thirty tons had gone up it, at low water, their shallop could not have got through.

At first the Pilgrims decided to settle in the Kingston area but they changed their minds when they became frightened of another Indian attack. Winslow also complained that this place was too far from their fishing spots; fishing was their principal means of making the profit they were under contract to do. He also claimed that it was so surrounded in thick bush that they would be in great danger of the Indians especially as their number were so little and there was so much ground to clear before they could feel safe.

Once again their settlement plans bogged down in debate and more research trips. Some of them wanted to settle opposite Plymouth in the Duxbury Bay area and some wanted to stay where they were. Winslow said some of them then crossed the bay five or six miles over and found an isle about two miles long which was wooded but had no fresh water. This breakaway group argued that this remote island would be the best spot because it was so easy to defend and offered great security.

After hours of debate during the day and that night the Pilgrims at last made up their minds. That night, they returned to the ship determined to make a start the next morning somewhere on the mainland.

20 December

With people shivering in the confined space below decks on the *Mayflower* and weakened by diseases from the infected air, the time had come for the Pilgrim leaders to take a stand. Their food stocks were running out and, what seemed to them even worse, their supply of beer was now dangerously low. So they narrowed the choice down to two places and decided to act boldly in the morning. After they had called on God for direction, they went ashore again to inspect the two places they thought most fitting.

According to Winslow, after landing and viewing the two places as well as they could, they came to the conclusion by majority vote to settle on the high ground, where there was a great deal of land cleared. This had been planted with corn three or four years ago and there was a brook running under the hillside with many delicate springs of good water. The water was deep enough to moor the boats there as well and there were many good fish. Also, on the further side of the river, a good deal of corn ground had been cleared.

Most of the Pilgrims were pleased with their choice, especially as nearby Burial Hill would give them such a commanding aspect over their surroundings. Winslow said that in one field there was a great hill on which they agreed to make a platform and to establish a fort with their guns which would command 'all round about'. From there they could see into the Bay and out to sea with a clear view of Cape Cod.

In fact there seemed to be few drawbacks apart from finding dry fuel for fire. Winslow predicted that their greatest labor would be fetching the wood, which was a quarter of a mile away. At least the Indians did not seem to be a problem. Having made the decision to settle at this spot twenty people were selected to go ashore the next day and to start to build houses.

21 December   The Pilgrims spent the day on the boat sorting out their equipment.

The weather deteriorated and Winslow wrote that it was so stormy and wet that they could not go ashore. They could do nothing. The climate could not have been less welcoming and, all that night, it blew hard and rained. It was so tempestuous that the shallop could not even land, let alone ferry supplies to the shore.

Finally, the shallop was able to get off with provisions and was able to reach shore. But it could not return because the wind blew so strongly.

Meanwhile Richard Britterige died. Unfortunately he could not be buried for two days because of stormy weather. His death reduced their numbers to ninety-four.

22 December   Their plans to begin building were then upset by yet another storm. Those still on the *Mayflower* could not get onto land, while those on land could not get back on board.

During the height of this storm goodwife Mary Allerton was delivered of a son. Ominously, it was still-born.

23 December   Winslow wrote that everyone was willing to start work on the settlement and, as the weather improved, a building party went ashore and felled and carried timber, to provide themselves 'stuff' for building.

Meanwhile the women mourned for the dead baby and comforted Mary Allerton; they made preparations to take the tiny body ashore to be buried along with that of Richard Britterige.

24 December   The Sabbath called a halt to the building program. All the Pilgrims attended prayer services, thanked God for their deliverance and for guiding them to Plymouth, and prayed for guidance for the building task they were to start the next day.

During the day the more nervous Pilgrims took fright, Winslow said, when some of the people on shore heard a cry from some hidden savages. The guards raised the alarm and all those on shore stood on their guard, expecting an assault. But all was quiet.

Another child, Solomon Prower, died on board the *Mayflower* while waiting to move ashore into a warm and clean home. His death reduced their numbers to ninety-three.

25 December   Then on Christmas Day — which to the Pilgrims had little of the significance it has for latter day Americans — they finally made a start on the first houses. Bradford reported that 'the 25 day begane to erecte the first house for commone use to receive them and their goods'. This twenty-foot-square house was initially to house people sleeping ashore and to be a store house for the food supplies. Winslow said it was a busy scene on shore — some felling timber, some sawing wood, some carrying. He said no man rested all that day.

As darkness fell and storm clouds developed they once again feared an Indian attack; towards night, some of them heard a noise which they feared was Indians. This sent them all diving for their muskets, but as they heard no further noises they relaxed their guard. Some of the party went back on board for the night leaving a small guard on shore at the building site. Winslow said that night they had another fearful storm of wind and rain.

The festive occasion did not escape totally unnoticed, however. Winslow admitted a certain amount of 'seduction' by the ship's Captain. He said that on the Monday, Christmas Day, they drank water on board for most of the day but, at night, the Master encouraged them to have some beer.

26 December   The Pilgrims had made an energetic start on their settlement, but this day bad weather again brought progress to a halt. Winslow said it was such foul weather that they could not even go ashore. Instead, they 'wasted' the day discussing their building plans and the layout of the settlement.

27 December   The weather fined up. Winslow said they clambered into the boat and went to work again, cutting down trees for uprights, splitting logs into planks and digging holes for uprights.

28 December   With another fine day the Pilgrim builders were able to make some progress sinking uprights and starting to build the walls of their dwellings.

Having selected Burial Hill as a focal point for their town center because, as Winslow explained, it had a good view and they could easily build a fortress around it for protection, the Pilgrims then designed a town on the seaside just below this protective hill. Leyden Street was to be the main thoroughfare and houses either side would face each other.

Winslow wrote that in the afternoon, they went to measure out the grounds. Then they calculated how many families there were, persuading all single men to join a family of their choice so that they might build fewer houses. When this was done it reduced the Pilgrim groups to nineteen families.

Although family households got more land than single men, all the Pilgrims received land grants which were allocated on a democratic basis. Single men got house block frontages of a little over eight feet with a depth of nearly fifty feet. The larger families were allotted bigger plots, but every person received half a pole in breadth, and three in length. Having agreed on this, lots were then cast and the land allocations were staked out.

The land grants were small given the space available but, as Winslow explained, they were feeling weaker by now and wanted to make sure they could erect protective barricades around their homes, so they kept the area as small as possible. He said most of them thought this proportion was large enough to begin with for houses and gardens. By now many of them were growing ill. In fact, having waited on the cold and cramped ship infecting each other with their ailments, they were now in no fit state to come ashore in midwinter to start constructing houses out of the forest. That would have been a major job at the best of times. From the very first delay in leaving England, their program had been put back and back to the point where they were founding the colony at the very worst possible time of year.

29 December The boat was sent ashore with the building party but once again bad weather soon stopped work, forcing them to spend more time cooped up on the *Mayflower*.

30 December Winslow wrote that however much they had prepared themselves for their labor, their people on shore were much troubled and discouraged with the constant rain and cold. The Indians by contrast were apparently keeping warm, as Winslow reported they saw great smokes of fire about six or seven miles from them.

31 December The weather improved but again storms blew up and it rained. As it was the Sabbath, they made no further progress on that day. All they could do was pray and watch the winter setting in.

1 January 1621 Although the disease which was affecting the Pilgrims during this first winter has never been clearly identified, it is likely that most of them were dying from either scurvy or pneumonia or a combination of both. Their diet was grossly inadequate and the extreme cold took its toll. Many of them had been weak even on departure and with inadequate food would have deteriorated further during the journey. With few warm clothes and weeks crowded together in an unhealthy, unventilated ship, they easily succumbed to disease and cold.

The Pilgrims would have done much better if they could have brought the *Mayflower* a bit closer to shore, Winslow claimed. They were hindered in lying so far off from the land, but their ship drew so much water that she lay a mile and a half away which meant that they took a long time in coming ashore each time and got very wet and cold in the process.

3 January The fires in the distance continued to intrigue them. Winslow related that some of the Pilgrims went abroad to gather thatch and saw more great fires of the Indians. Once again they saw their cornfields but saw no Indians themselves, nor had they seen any of them since coming to the bay in which they had decided to settle.

4 January The Pilgrims could not bear the tension any longer. They had to make contact with their neighbors, so they sent out yet another mission. However this new expedition of peace brought nothing back except a little extra food. Winslow related how Captain Myles Standish, with four or five more, went to see if they could meet with any of the savages in the place where the fires had been made. They went into some of their houses but found all empty. As they came home, they shot an eagle which Winslow said was excellent meat hardly to be discerned from mutton.

5 January A stray fish then highlighted their lack of essential equipment, such as fish hooks. Winslow wrote that one of the sailors found a herring alive upon the shore which the Master had for his supper and this reminded the Pilgrims of their lack of a fresh fish diet; they had only managed to catch one single cod all that time for want of small hooks.

6 January As the winter set in more of the Pilgrims were falling sick and dying. Winslow reported that Master Martin was very sick and, to their judgment, had no hope of living; consequently Master Carver was sent to return on board to speak with him, as Christopher Martin was the Company's treasurer. John Carver came the next morning to organize the Pilgrim's books before the treasurer died.

8 January As it appeared to be a fine day Winslow said Master Jones sent the shallop out into the bay to see if they could catch some fish. Unfortunately, the weather turned against them yet again and they had to battle a great storm out at sea and were forced to take shelter on a nearby island. That night however they returned with three seals which they had caught and an excellent cod. This at least assured them that they should have plenty of fish shortly.

Back on the *Mayflower* both Christopher Martin and then Digory Priest had died, further reducing the Pilgrim numbers. As the bitter cold month of January progressed the Pilgrims found their number reduced to less than ninety.

A new and exciting discovery was then made, when the Pilgrims tracked down Billington Sea. Winslow related how Francis Billington, having the week before seen from the top of a tree on a high hill a 'great sea', went with one of the Master's Mates to explore it. They went three miles and then came to an expanse of water divided into two great lakes. They claimed that in their estimation these lakes were full of fine fresh water with plenty of fish and fowl.

Winslow said that on this exploring party Billington and his companion also found seven or eight Indian houses, once again all empty. When they first saw the houses they were in some fear as there were only the two of them and they only had one gun.

9 January   The Pilgrim building brigade had now been working on land for more than two weeks and now at last they had almost finished the community storehouse.

Their next step was to sit down and plan the individual homes. They based this program on the fundamental American principle of each man working for himself. Winslow said it was a reasonable day and so they began the building of their town, designing at first two rows of houses for safety reasons. Then they agreed at a meeting that every man should build his own house thinking, by that course, men would make more haste than working in common.

By then the Common House, in which they had their meetings, was all but finished and needed only covering. It was about twenty-feet square.

11 January   On this day, catastrophe nearly struck the official scribe himself — William Bradford. If he had died future generations might never have known what happened when the Pilgrims founded America because, although Winslow kept a good record, Bradford was the only one to keep the records from the start to the finish, not dying till 1657.

Winslow said William Bradford was hard at work building his own house frame in sunshine when he was suddenly and vehemently struck down by a great pain in his hip-bone. He was in such agony writhing on the ground that his fellow Pilgrims doubted that he would live.

Bradford was taken indoors and given food and drink and treated with what remedies were to hand. He had suffered extreme cold in the different exploration trips he had taken part in, especially the last one, and although he had never complained, had since these trips felt great pains in his ankles. Now this had spread to his hip.

Bradford grew a little better towards night Winslow said and in time, 'through God's mercy', recovered.

12 January   Just as the general storehouse was almost finished, bad weather once again stopped work.

Another cause for concern arose, too. Two Pilgrims wandered off and became lost in the woods. Winslow said that these two people caused 'great sorrow and care'. Four people had been sent to gather and cut thatch in the morning. Two of them, John Goodman and Peter Browne, decided to move to another site further into the woods and asked the other two to follow after binding up that thatch which was cut. But when the two went after them they could not find them anywhere, nor hear anything of them at all even though they shouted as loud as they could. Eventually they returned to the colony and reported their disappearance.

Everybody was anxious. These were the first people to go missing; perhaps the Indians had kidnapped the two missing men. The Pilgrim leader Master Carver and four others then went to look for them, but had no luck in finding Goodman and Browne. They had to return empty-handed before night fell.

13 January At first light another group was sent out to try and find the two lost men. Winslow said they armed ten or twelve men, thinking the Indians had surprised the two men. But once again they could neither see nor hear anything at all.

Eventually Goodman and Browne stumbled back into the settlement. They explained that they had just lost their way, having strolled off for a walk at lunch time taking their meat to refresh themselves. On going a little way they found a lake where their mastiff and spaniel raised a deer. The dogs chased it and they followed and in the process they got lost.

They wandered about all that afternoon, becoming very wet and at night nearly dying from the cold when it began to snow. They had few clothes and no weapons, apart from a sickle, nor any victuals. Unable to find their way back they walked up and down looking for shelter but could not even find a deserted Indian house.

The two lost men then decided to spend the night camped in a tree. They were terrified because they heard what they thought were two 'lions' roaring and a third 'lion' they thought was very near them.

It was a lesson to them all not to go out into the woods alone, unarmed and without supplies. From then on everyone was instructed to tell the leaders when they were going even for a walk. With their numbers declining every day through sickness, the Pilgrims could not afford to lose people unnecessarily.

The return of the lost men set the Pilgrims talking for some days. Goodman and Browne had in fact experienced something of an ordeal. Winslow said that next day they remained at the tree's root, so that, if the 'lions' came, they might climb back up to safety. Winslow believed their dogs frightened off the wolves and concluded that it pleased God to keep the wild beasts away from the two. They were only able to find their way back by climbing up a hill and from there spotting the two islands in the bay to pinpoint the colony.

One thing that came out of the mishap was that the lost men had discovered some new areas of useful land. As soon as it was light, they took their companions back to these good locations and passed by many lakes, brooks and woods. Winslow said the land was good, especially in one place where the Indians had burnt an area of ground about five miles in length, which was fine and level country.

14 January Another blow now struck the new settlement. Ironically on the first Sabbath that they were able to observe on shore, the main building they had painstakingly constructed was damaged by fire. According to Winslow they first realized the fire had started when they saw the smoke from the *Mayflower*. He said that in the morning, at about six o'clock, they came on deck as the ship was battered by a very great wind and they saw the building on fire. He described this as a new 'discomfort'.

As no Pilgrims were out and about that early, they understandably blamed the Indians. Winslow said they soon discovered that the Indians were not to blame, however, as on landing, they realized that the house was set on fire by a spark that flew into the thatch.

Some Pilgrims had been asleep inside the building at the time, including Governor Carver and Bradford who was still bedridden from his illness. Winslow described how they would have died if they had not risen with 'good speed', because they could have been blown up with the gunpowder stored indoors.

Others could also have died in the fire because at the time this 'common house' was being used as a temporary and overcrowded hospital for the sick and dying. Winslow said it was full of beds end-to-end.

15 January The day after the fire the heavens opened as if to prevent the possibility of further sparks. Winslow lamented that it rained all day; the people on ship board could not go on shore and those on shore could not do any labor because it was so wet.

More people continued to fall sick in the wet and cold weather. The Pilgrims were still without proper shelter and the number of dead continued to mount. Some were buried in the little graveyard that had been established on Burial Hill.

16 January Fine weather enabled them to start work again. Initially they had to clean up the ruined 'common house' and clear away the blackened debris.

17 January Another fine day enabled them to begin rebuilding the burnt out building and resume work on their individual homes.

18 January Winslow said it was a warm day of sunshine, more like spring than winter. Those people in good health worked cheerfully.

19 January The Pilgrim builders now decided they needed a larger common house for supplies, so in spite of more bad weather, made a start on a new shelter. Winslow said they held a meeting where they resolved to make this 'Shed' because there were too many supplies for one common house; already there were supplies sitting on shore. Most of the day, however, it rained and they could not work.

Here Winslow described how the ill-fated John Goodman — whose feet were still suffering from the time he got lost — now went for another walk a short way from the settlement. He had with him a little spaniel. Two wolves, seeing the dog, ran after it. The dog fled to Goodman for protection but he did not have anything to protect even himself with. He picked up a stick and threw it at them, managing to hit one. That didn't stop them; indeed it was only when he managed to find a stout 'piece of paling' that they stopped harassing him and the dog. The two wolves just sat on their tails, 'grinning' at him for a time before finally trotting off.

21 January As usual the faithful Pilgrims kept the Sabbath but this time they could hold their meeting on land. With an increasing number of Pilgrims falling sick and dying in the cold and wet exposed settlement, Elder Brewster prayed for a halt to the deaths that were depleting the settlement. Soon there would not be enough men to form a proper guard.

22 January Winslow wrote that the building program continued successfully despite the sick and dying and they were at last able to move food into the new storehouse. He said it was a fair day, so they were also able to work on their own houses.

24 January According to Winslow the Pilgrims now had a series of a good building days. He reported that the rest of the week they 'followed their business' with great energy.

29 January More supplies were brought ashore. Winslow said the day started out in the morning with cold frost and sleet but after warm sun became reasonably fair. Both the long boat and the shallop brought their common goods on shore.

Sadly, back on the *Mayflower*, the wife of Captain Standish, Mistress Rose, died.

30 January The building continued despite freezing weather. Another Pilgrim passed away.

31 January Winslow said it was such a cold day with so much sleet that they could not work. January had been a terrible month, during which many of their people had died and now they were less than seventy.

Then at last the Pilgrims caught a glimpse of their Plymouth neighbors. Winslow described that in the morning the Master and some others saw two Indians on the island near their ship. What they had come for, they could not tell. The Indians retreated as fast as they appeared and the Pilgrims were not able to speak with them.

4 February The bad weather continued and now threatened the partially-empty *Mayflower*. Winslow said it was very wet and rainy with the greatest gusts of wind that they had ever had since arriving. Although they rode in a very good harbor, the ship was in great danger because, with the goods taken off, she lacked ballast. She began to be blown about at her anchor dangerously.

The stormy weather also caused much daubing of their houses to fall down.

9 February The bad conditions continued. More people died. But Winslow said as long as the bad weather continued they could do little work and were unable to construct all the warm shelters that were necessary.

When bad weather was not undermining their efforts other calamaties seemed to befall them. Once again a fire broke out in the roof of a hut they were using to shelter some of their sick people. This time however they were able to act much faster and the fire was put out before any great harm was done.

On a better note, Captain Jones bagged some game. He shot five geese which he kindly distributed among the sick people. He found also a deer killed by the Indians who had cut off the horns and although a wolf was eating it when he came across it, he still brought it home.

11 February The Pilgrims had now been in Cape Cod Harbor for two months. They had found a suitable place for their settlement and, despite the house fires, had made a good start building substantial community and private homes — but the cost of the various delays was proving enormous. So many more deaths occurred during this period that they began to fear for their survival as a group.

16 February Although it was a fair day, the northerly wind continued as did the frost. Winslow related that in the afternoon one of their people went looking for fowls. Having taken up position in the reeds by the creek side about a mile and a half from the Plantation, he saw twelve Indians, marching towards their settlement. Also in the woods, he heard the noise of 'many more'.

He lay quietly till they had passed and then ran back to raise the alarm. All the Pilgrims fell back into the settlement and armed themselves. They waited, but the Indians did not show up.

Following this, they had their first possessions stolen by the Indians. Winslow wrote that Captain Myles Standish and Francis Cooke, having been working in the woods, returned home for lunch and left their tools

Contemporary drawing of an Indian dancer, labelled 'The flyer'.

behind them. When they returned they discovered their tools had been taken away, so in future they decided to be more on their guard and to keep their guns always ready to fire.

With more Pilgrims dying and the survivors getting weaker and weaker, fear began to spread through the settlement now that the Indians seemed so close. Some of the Pilgrims were getting so frightened that they wanted to go back to the *Mayflower* and so, after a meeting with the leaders, it was decided to form a proper guard responsible for protecting the colony. Winslow said that in the morning, they called a meeting to establish 'military orders' among themselves. They selected Myles Standish as their Captain and gave him authority of command in such affairs. Having served in the English military forces, Standish was well versed in traditional military practices and procedures. As time passed he taught his fellow Pilgrims the basic arts of handling weapons and forming defensive positions in case of enemy attack.

It was Bradford's opinion that, having made a good start on building the settlement, this was the next important milestone in the settlement's history: 'And after they had provided a place for their goods, or comone store, (which were long in unlading for want of boats, foulness of winter weather, and sicknes) and begun some small cottages for their habitation, as time would admitte, they mette and consulted of lawes & orders, both for their civill & military Governmente, as the necessitie of their condition did require, still adding therunto as urgent occasion in severall times, and as cases did require'.

Now if the Indians did attack they would be prepared.

With all the setbacks to the building program, the delays in establishing the settlement and the continual threat of Indian attack, factions inevitably formed. Many of them, seeing their brothers and sisters dying around them, were terrified that they might be the next to die. Bradford wrote: 'In these hard & difficult beginings they found some discontents & murmurings arise amongst some, and mutinous speeches & carriags in other; but they were soone quelled & overcome by the wisdome, patience, and just & equal carrage of things by the Govenor and better part, which clave faithfully togeather in the maine.'

The continuing death toll was nevertheless alarming.

28 February

By the end of February the death toll had reached a peak. With as many as two or three people dying a day it was not long before half of their original number lay dead and buried beneath the frozen ground. Bradford: 'But that which was most sadd & lamentable was, that in 2 or 3 moneths time, halfe of their company dyed, espetially in January & February, being the depth of winter, and wanting houses & other comforts; being infected with the scurvie & other diseases, which this long vioage & their inacomodate condition had brought upon them; so as ther dyed some times 2 or 3 of a day, in the foresaid time; that of 100 & odd persons, scarce 50 remained'.

It was a terrible time for the fifty survivors. If there was any possible comfort in this, it was, in Bradford's thinking, that the tragedy brought out the best in some of the Pilgrims: 'And of these in the time of most distres, ther was but 6 or 7 sound persons, who, to their great comendations be it spoken, spared no pains, night nor day, but with abundance of toyle and hazard of their owne health, fetched them woode, made them fires, drest them meat, made their beds, washed their lothsome cloaths, cloathed & uncloathed them; in a word, did all the homly & necessarie offices for them which dainty & quesie stomacks cannot endure to hear named; and all this willingly & cherfully, without any grudging in the least, shewing herein their true love unto their friends & bretheren. A rare example & worthy to be remembred'.

Bradford wrote that the two most heroic were the religious Elder and the Military Captain: 'Two of these 7 were Mr. William Brewster, ther reverend Elder, & Myles Standish, ther Captein & military comander, unto whom my selfe, & many others, were much beholden in our low & sicke condition. And yet the Lord so upheld these persons, as in this general calamity they were not at all infected either with sicknes, or lamnes. And what I have said of these, I may say of many others who dyed in this generall vissitation, & others yet living, that whilst they had health, yea, or any strength continuing, they were not wanting to any that had need of them. And I doubte not but their recompence is with the Lord'.

By contrast to the Pilgrims, the ship's crew behaved quite badly during this tragic period, both towards one another and the Pilgrims: 'But I may not hear pass by an other remarkable passage not to be forgotten. As this calamitie fell among the passengers that were to be left here to plant, and were hasted a shore and made to drinke water, that the sea-men might have the more bear, and one in his sickness desiring but a small cann of beere, it was answered, that if he were their owne father he should have none; the disease begane to fall amongst them also, so as allmost halfe of their company dyed before they went away, and many of their officers and lustyest men, as the boatson, gunner, 3 quarter-maisters, the cooke, & others'.

The situation further deteriorated because the unprincipled sailors abandoned their diseased shipmates as they fell sick, leaving them to die in agony: 'At which the master was something strucken and sent sick a shore and tould the Govr he should send for beer for them that had need of it, though he drunke water homward bound. But now amongst his company ther was farr another kind of carriage in this miserie then amongst the passengers; for they that before had been boone companions in drinking & joyllity in the time of their health & wellfare, begane now to deserte one another in this calamitie, saing they would not hasard ther lives for them, they should be infected by coming to help them in their cabins, and so, after they came to dye by it, would doe little or nothing for them, but if they dyed let them dye'.

Some of the sailors who were striken by disease were inspired by the Pilgrims' humanity, Bradford claimed: 'But shuch of the passengers as were yet abord shewed them what mercy they could, which made some of their harts relente, as the boatson (& some others), who was a prowd yonge man, and would often curse & scofe at the passengers; but when he grew weak, they had compassion on him and helped him; then he confessed he did not deserve it at their hands, he had abused them in word & deed. O! saith he, you, I now see, shew your love like Christians indeed one to another, but we let one another lye & dye like doggs'.

However, for others, there seemed to be no bounds to their evil behavior: 'Another lay cursing his wife, saing if it had not ben for her he had never come this unlucky viage, and anone cursing his felows, saing he had done this & that, for some of them, he had spente so much, & so much, amongst them, and they were now weary of him, and did not help him, having need. Another gave his companion all he had, if he died, to help him in his weaknes; he went and got a litle spise & made him a mess of meat once or twise, and because he dyed not so soone as he expected, he went amongst his fellows, & swore the rogue would cuse him, he would see him choaked before he made him any more meate; and yet the pore fellow dyed before morning'.

1 March Bradford, who is the only authority on the great sickness, recorded that those who were struck down by the general sickness included Roger Wilder, Jasper More, a Boy who was the brother of Richard More, Elizabeth Winslow, Elias Story, Ellen More, Mary Allerton, John Hooke, John Crakston, Rose Standish, Christopher Martin, Marie Martin, Solomon Prower, John Langmore, William Mullins, Alice Mullins, Joseph Mullins, Robert Carter, William White, William Holbeck, Edward Thompson, Edward Tilley, Ann Tilley, John Tilley, Mistress Tilley, Thomas Rogers, Thomas Tinker, Mistress Tinker, Master Tinker, John Rigsdale, Alice Rigsdale, James Chilton, Susanna Chilton, Edward Fuller, Mistress Fuller, John Turner, Master Turner (1), Master Turner (2), Sarah Eaton, Moses Fletcher, John Goodman, Thomas Williams, Digory Priest, Edmund Margesson, Richard Britteridge, Richard Clarke, John Allerton, Thomas English.

It was also difficult for the survivors who at times were digging graves and burying up to two or three corpses a day in the cold hard earth beneath the midwinter snow. By March almost half the people who left England six months earlier now lay buried. Now only the truly resolute could survive.

In fact, it was remarkable that any of them were able to survive until the arrival of the first relief ship the following November. They were a vulnerable little band. Apart from the cold, shortage of food, disease and difficulty raising crops, there was now the additional threat from the Indians who could have wiped them out in one attack.

It was therefore ironic that their survival was to depend on these very Indians, as in the spring, the local Indians took pity on them and, led by a young Brave called Squanto, came to their rescue.

8 Brave Squanto to the Rescue

March 1621–January 1622

Afterwards they (as many as were able)
began to plant ther corne, in which
servise Squanto stood them in great
stead, showing them both the maner how
to set it, and after how to dress & tend it.
William Bradford

3 March 1621 At last, after the terrible winter of death, the early signs of spring appeared and the Pilgrims stopped dying. A grateful Bradford wrote: 'the Spring now approaching, it pleased God the mortalitie begane to cease amongst them, and the sick and lame recovered apace, which put as it were new life into them; though they had borne their sadd affliction with much patience & contentednes'.

Winslow said that on the third of March the wind came from the south and the morning was misty, but towards noon they had warm and fair weather; the birds sang in the woods most pleasantly. The season of rebirth had come at last putting an end to the misery that had killed off half the Pilgrims and the eyes of the little band of survivors must have filled with tears of joy as the first spring flowers burst out through the melting snows.

Not that the first Pilgrim spring brought perfect weather. On the same day, Winslow said that at one o'clock the skies filled with thunder for the first time since they had landed and after an hour it rained very 'sadly' till midnight.

5 March The warmer weather also brought danger as now the Indians would become more adventurous. The Pilgrims prepared themselves to fight. Bradford said they had seen the first Plymouth Indians as early as 16 February 'skulking about the settlement' and 'once they stoale away their tools wher they had been at worke, & were gone to diner'. He believed that the better weather would encourage the Indians to attack.

102

Governor John Carver and other Pilgrim leaders ask for guidance from above as they draw up and sign the Mayflower Compact on board the ship, shortly after arriving in the new land.

Once the Pilgrims had built their Community Hall they were able to hold their first full prayer service on shore.

*Having befriended the Pilgrims the Indian brave Squanto then served
as their guide on a number of exploring and hunting expeditions.*

*Day after day the Pilgrims waited anxiously for the return of their
Mayflower, but it was nearly a year before a second ship brought a new
wave of settlers to the colony.*

Before long cod fishing became an important industry in Cape Cod Harbor with Pilgrims and other settlers drying and salting the fish to supplement their tables and their incomes.

As the years went by Plymouth Harbor proved to be a popular port of call for an increasing number of ships developing trade between the Old World and the New.

Some of the Pilgrims were eventually buried on Burial Hill which overlooks the first landfall in Cape Cod Harbor.

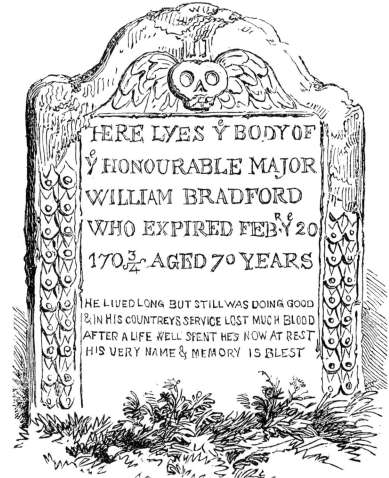

HERE LYES Y BODY OF
Y HONOURABLE MAJOR
WILLIAM BRADFORD
WHO EXPIRED FEB·Y 20
170 3/4 AGED 70 YEARS

HE LIVED LONG BUT STILL WAS DOING GOOD
& IN HIS COUNTREYS SERVICE LOST MUCH BLOOD
AFTER A LIFE WELL SPENT HE'S NOW AT REST
HIS VERY NAME & MEMORY IS BLEST

William Bradford's tombstone. He lived to the ripe old age of 70.

They had created a proper guard and begun to train themselves, but so far without much success, because each time they assembled for military practise they were interrupted.

Bradford recounted how they had tried it first on 17 February 'calling a meeting for the establishing of military orders' and choosing Captain Standish as the leader but two Indians had appeared on top of a nearby hill inviting the Pilgrims to come and meet with them before then suddenly disappearing into the woods. The contact was getting closer and closer every day and the Pilgrims were getting nervous. They had even transferred one of the larger guns from the *Mayflower* to the shore on 21 February, and mounted this up on Burial Hill as a defence for the settlement.

Bradford reported that 'All this while the Indians came skulking about them, and would sometimes show them selves aloofe of, but when any aproached near them, they would rune away'.

7 March Life went on however and the business of cultivating the ground began to become important as the weather warmed up. The Governor gave the Pilgrims a lead by setting out on a fishing expedition. Winslow reported that Master Carver, with five others, went to the great ponds, which although it was near where Indians had been seen, seemed to be excellent fishing places. Also, others began planting, and some garden seeds were sown.

16 March As it was a fairly warm day and the Pilgrims had made good progress on their buildings and planted many of their seeds, they decided it was time to get back to the business of protecting themselves. Winslow said they held a meeting and agreed to finalize their defence strategy and create a set of Military Orders.

This was their second attempt to form the permanent guard and to work out emergency procedures but unbelievably they were disturbed again by the very people whom they were arming against. Winslow said that while they were going through their military instructions an Indian 'presented himself'. This caused an alarm, especially as he very boldly walked up all alone, through their houses, and straight up to them.

The Pilgrims stopped him, issuing a challenge — asking him who he was and where he thought he was going.

Immediately they confronted him, it became obvious that he was a friend and not a foe. Winslow said this Indian replied by saluting them in English, and bade them 'Welcome!'. It turned out he had learned some broken English from Englishmen who had come in the past to fish at Monhegan, an island twelve miles off the Maine coast between Penobscot and Kennebec. The Indian told the Pilgrims his name was Samoset.

Bradford said Samoset 'spoke to them in broken English, which they could well understand, but marvelled at it'. Then 'at length they understood by discourse with him, that he was not of these parts, but belonged to the eastene parts, wher some English ships came to fhish, with whom he was aquainted, & could name sundrie of them by their names, amongst whom he had gott his language'.

From the start Bradford said Samoset was useful to the Pilgrims and 'became proftable to them in aquainting them with many things concerning the state of the cuntry in the east-parts wher he lived, which was afterwards profitable unto them; as also of the people hear, of their names, number, & strength; of their situation & distance from this place, and who was cheefe amongst them'.

Samoset became their first real friend. Winslow described him as a man who spoke freely and had many stories to tell. He had a seemly carriage and was a tall, good-looking man. As he was the first 'savage' they met, Samoset fascinated the curious Pilgrims greatly, especially as they had been waiting so long to make contact with the local inhabitants.

Samoset told the amazed Pilgrims his dramatic life story. He came from a part of Maine that had been visited by English fishermen for years and had spent a lot of time getting to know them and their language. He had then heard about the arrival of the Pilgrims and had for some time been travelling south to meet them. Winslow said that Samoset came from Morattigon and was a native of Pemaquid, the area now occupied by the modern town of Bristol, Maine.

Samoset was evidently more than a casual acquaintance of the English as he was invited on board the ship of an English fishing expedition under Captain Dermer at Monhegan, where he had spent some time with another Indian, called Squanto, whom he claimed was even more of a friend of the English. At one time Squanto had apparently sailed off on Captain Dermer's ship across the ocean.

Bradford said that Samoset claimed Squanto had even been to England and back: 'the other Indian whos name was Squanto, a native of this place, had been in England & could speake better English then him selfe'. The Pilgrims, finding it difficult to believe, replied they wanted to know more and meet this well-travelled Squanto some day.

Winslow said that as the wind was beginning to rise a little, they cast a horseman's coat about Samoset for he was stark naked with only a piece of leather about his waist, which had a fringe about a span long or little more. He also had a bow, and two arrows — one headed, and the other unheaded. The hair on his head was black and worn long behind and short in front, with none on his face at all, 'being clean shaven.'

Samoset had evidently acquired a taste for a few European indulgences, as Winslow recounted that he asked for some beer. The Pilgrims gave him some 'strong water' instead and a biscuit with butter and cheese along with some pudding and a piece of a mallard — all of which he liked very much.

Over this meal Samoset revealed the terrible truth about the dreadful plague that had been brought to New England by the Europeans who were infected with smallpox and had spread this disease among the Indians some years earlier. Samoset claimed this had decimated the Indian population. Winslow said that Samoset told them that the place where the Indians now lived was called Patuxet but, about four years ago, all the inhabitants in the Plymouth area had died of this extraordinary plague. That explained why the Pilgrims had found none.

Now the Pilgrims understood the reasons for all the crowded graves they had been digging up in the Cape Cod and Provincetown area. At the same time they took heart because it seemed they were not occupying Indian land as a result, because as Winslow said, now there were no people to hinder their possession, or to lay claim unto it.

Obviously at home in English company and enjoying the attention he was getting, Samoset was keen to stay in the settlement. Winslow wrote that they would gladly have got rid of him but he was not willing to go even at night so, not without some suspicion, they lodged him at Stephen Hopkins's house and watched over him.

17 March   Winslow said that in the morning they dismissed Samoset and gave him a knife, a bracelet, and a ring. He went away, back to the Massasoits from whence, he said, he came.

Samoset had blamed other tribes for stealing from the Pilgrims and said he knew who had stolen their tools and would try and get them back for the Pilgrims. Thus the first real Indian contact had proved to be a good one and the Pilgrims hoped to build on this friendship.

18 March   In the middle of the Sabbath, Samoset returned — but this time with some friends. They had come in peace as Bradford said: 'he came againe, & 5 more with him, & they brought again all the tooles that were stolen away before'.

Winslow said that Samoset brought with him five other tall and strong men. Every man had a deer's skin on him and the leader had a wild cat's skin, or such like, on one arm. Most of them had long hose up to their groins which was tightly woven. Above their groins up to their waist they wore another leather garment. He claimed they looked altogether like Irish trousers.

This first close-up encounter with a group of Indians enabled the Pilgrims to study their hitherto elusive hosts. Winslow reported that their complexion was like English gypsies. They had no hair, or very little hair, on their faces and on their heads had long hair down to their shoulders. Their hair styles varied with some being only cut at the front, some trussed up in front of the face with a feather, others with their hair shaped like a fan and still others with their hair like a fox's tail hanging out.

As Samoset had proved to be a friend the Pilgrims extended the welcome to his friends as well. Winslow said they gave the group the entertainment they thought was fitting. The Indians ate liberally of the English victuals and made it clear to the Pilgrims that they wanted friendship. They sang and danced after their manner, going through many different 'antics'.

The Indians then introduced the Pilgrims to their tobacco smoking culture. Winslow said that one of the Indians had a little tobacco in a bag which he took out and used but none of the Pilgrims smoked it. The Pilgrims were also amazed by the Indian's decorations as some of them had their faces painted black, from the forehead to the chin.

Used to trading with Englishmen, the Indians had brought goods to swap, not realizing of course that no commercial activities could take place in the Pilgrim settlement on a Sunday. Winslow said that they brought three or four skins, but the Pilgrims would not trade at all that day. Bradford added: 'they brought againe all the tooles that were stolen away before', and as this was a gesture of friendship, the Pilgrims gladly received them.

But it was not long before the Pilgrims had had enough of this ungodly interruption to their holy day and so, Winslow said, because it was Sunday they dismissed the Indians as soon as they could ... although they did give every one of them some trifles.

Although most of the Indians left they could not get rid of Samoset as easily as that. Winslow said that Samoset was either sick, or 'feigned himself' so and would not go away with the others. Indeed, he insisted on staying with the Pilgrims till the Wednesday morning.

Bradford thought this five man Indian mission would pave the way for a future peace treaty meeting with the local Indian chief as it 'made way for the coming of their great Sachem, called Massasoyt; who, about 4 or 5 days after, came with the cheefe of his freinds & other attendance, with the aforesaid Squanto. With whom, after frendly entertainment, & some gifts given him, they made a peace with him'.

19 March   Left alone by the Indians and enjoying fair days, the Pilgrims got on with planting their corn and continued building their homes.

20 March   Winslow said that, as this also proved a fair day, they dug their grounds and sowed more of their garden seeds.

21 March   The Pilgrims were finally able to persuade their Indian friend to leave and Samoset walked off into the forest.

Now they were alone again they could get back to the military training. But according to Winslow this third attempt at establishing emergency procedures was unbelievably frustrated by the enemy again. They had just convened a meeting to formulate the regulations needed to protect themselves and to confirm the military strategy that was formerly propounded by Captain Standish when they were interrupted for the third time.

Suddenly out of the woods two or three 'savages' presented themselves and this time they were unknown and appeared more menacing. These Indians whetted and rubbed their arrows and strings and made a show of defiance. Winslow said Captain Standish and another man, with their muskets, went over the brook to them, followed by two of the seamen, but as they drew near, the Indians ran away.

This day was also an important one because, after over four months in the colony, they were able to bring the last of their people and possessions ashore from the *Mayflower*. Winslow said that with much ado, they got their Carpenter, who had been sick with scurvy for a long time, to prepare their shallop and to use this boat to fetch all the remaining people and possessions from the ship to the new settlement.

22 March   Another very fair, warm day enabled the Pilgrims to get on with building and planting, at least until they were interrupted once again by their new friends who reappeared out of the woods.

Winslow relayed that Samoset came again bringing with him Squanto, the Indian who had travelled overseas. They brought with them some skins to trade and some red herrings. As it turned out Squanto had only arrived back in the Plymouth area himself a year or so before from England, where he had been on a trip with a fishing ship under the command of Captain Dermer. On discussing his story further the Pilgrims learnt that Captain Dermer had persuaded Squanto to travel back to England to show the English what the Indians were like, in order to create confidence among future New England commercial traders and to teach the English people something of the Indian language. Squanto had then been brought back to Plymouth in late 1619. Dermer had probably saved Squanto's life, because, while he was away, the plague struck down most of his family and friends. When he landed back in Plymouth most of them were dead.

Squanto was now anxious to serve as a go-between and offered to introduce these new English visitors to his Chief, Massasoit. The Pilgrims eagerly accepted the invitation.

Winslow said that the Indian King then came to the top of a nearby hill, and had in train sixty men. Squanto went up to him and brought word that the Pilgrims should send one person to parley. Winslow himself then went and invited the Indians to trade in peace. He said the Pilgrims sent the King a pair of knives, and a copper chain with a jewel in it. The Pilgrims did not forget the Indian taste for good food and drink either; they sent such luxuries as brandy, biscuits and butter which were all willingly accepted.

Chief Massasoit seemed confident that these new arrivals had come in peace. Winslow said he came over the brook with some twenty men following him, leaving all their bows and arrows behind them. At this show of peace, Myles Standish and Isaac Allerton with a half a dozen musketeers went forward and met the King at the brook, and they conducted him to a house being built where they placed a green rug, and three or four cushions.

On Massasoit's arrival the Pilgrims drew out their trump card — the Governor himself — who greeted the Indian Chief with as much ceremony as the Pilgrims could muster. Winslow wrote that Governor John Carver entered with 'drum and trumpet after him', and some musketeers. After salutations, the Governor kissed Massasoit's hand, and the King then kissed him. They sat down to parley.

Massasoit and Carver then had the first powwow to draw up the terms and conditions for the two races to live together. During this negotiation session, Winslow said, the Governor called for some 'strong water' and drank the health of Massasoit.

Winslow asserted that Massasoit at first seemed frightened of Governor Carver, as all the while he sat by the Governor, he trembled for fear. This was curious because Massasoit was a very lusty man, in his best years and had an able body. He was of grave countenance and hardly ever spoke. He was impressive in his attire as he wore a great chain of white bone beads about his neck and behind his neck hung a little bag of tobacco which he smoked often.

Winslow also described Massasoit as appearing to have oiled both his head and face and that he looked very greasy. All his followers were likewise painted on their faces, in part or totally. Some were painted black, some red, some yellow, and some white; some were painted with crosses and other 'strange' symbols. Some Indians had skins on them and some were naked. The king had at his bosom, hanging on a string, a long knife. Winslow said Massasoit was amazed at their trumpet and some of his men tried to blow it as loudly as they could.

After some hours of negotiating, Carver and Massasoit solemnly announced that they had arrived at a treaty that they could both honor. Winslow said that after all was concluded, the impressive Massasoit and his retinue departed.

Not so Samoset and Squanto, however. They stayed all night with the Pilgrims. Meanwhile the King and all his men stayed all night in the woods with all their wives and women with them, not more than half a mile from the settlement.

The first negotiations had thus been a great success. Bradford said that 'they had made a peace with him' which 'proved to be a long-lasting treaty'.

The first Pilgrim/Indian treaty: 21 March 1621

Bradford recorded that these were the terms:

1. That neither he nor any of his, should injurie or doe hurte to any of their people.

2. That if any of his did any hurte to any of theirs, he should send the offender, that they might punish him.

3. That if any thing were taken away from any of theirs, he should

cause it to be restored; and they should doe the like to his.

4. If any did unjustly warr against him, they would aide him, if any did warr against them, he should aide them.

5. He should send to his neighbours confederats, to certifie them of this, that they might not wrong them, but might be likewise comprised in the conditions of peace.

6. That when ther men came to them, they should leave their bows & arrows behind them'. (Winslow recorded that it was also agreed the Pilgrims should do similarly with their pieces, when they came to the Indians.)

Lastly, Winslow said the Pilgrims added a promise that because the Indian Chief had agreed to sign the treaty, King James would esteem Massasoit as his friend and ally.

23 March The success of the first Pilgrim reception for the Indians was unqualified and before long the word spread to inspire many more Indians to come forward and enjoy their hospitality. For example, Winslow reported that the very next morning many Indians came to them hoping to get some free victuals.

That day, too, the Pilgrims were told that Massasoit wanted to return the hospitality. This was an important invitation, so Governor Carver selected Myles Standish and Isaac Allerton to go with him.

On visiting Massasoit, the Pilgrim delegates were made most welcome; Massasoit even gave them three or four groundnuts and some tobacco.

Fortunately by now, it appeared as if the Pilgrims and Indians were going to be friends because, as Winslow said, the Indians passed up many opportunities of killing defenceless Pilgrims. The Pilgrims themselves still found it difficult to conceive that Massasoit was willing to live in peace with them, yet his people had seen Pilgrims alone or in groups of two or three in the woods at work or fowling but had not harmed them.

With the Indians off their hands for the moment, the Pilgrims returned to the task of organizing their defences. They had tried three times to hold military parades and drill everyone on emergency procedures but each time the Indians had interrupted them. Now they wanted to sit down and draw up rules and regulations for a safer life in the colony. This was especially important to them at this point as, according to their old calendar, it was the arrival of spring. A new year had started and they wanted to start it off on the right foot.

This time they not only managed to have a long meeting and design a system of defence but they were also able to agree on the very first set of laws governing the new colony. Winslow recounted that they finalized both Military Orders and the basic Pilgrim set of Laws and Orders for government of the colony.

These laws became the Pilgrims' basis of government and lasted until

1636 when a new code of laws was formalized. This was eventually refined and then printed in 1671 as *The Book of the General Laws of the Inhabitants of New Plymouth*.

During this general assembly the Pilgrims confirmed their respect for John Carver by selecting him to lead them again.

Bradford recorded that their original Indian friend Samoset eventually got tired of living with them and 'he returned to his place caled Sowams, some 40 mile from this place' but Squanto 'continued with them, and was their interpreter, and was a spetiall instrument sent of God for their good beyond their expectation'.

With the food supplies running low it was important to sow seeds, fish successfully and catch live game in the woods — yet the Pilgrims were neither experienced nor familar with local conditions. Once he realized how inexperienced they actually were, Bradford said Squanto generously stepped forward and offered to help them. From that moment onwards serving the Pilgrims seemed to become Squanto's sole mission and 'He directed them how to set their corne, wher to take fish, and how to procure other comodities, and was also their pilott to bring them to unknowne places for their profitt, and never left them till he dyed'.

As Squanto spent longer with them, Bradford wrote, they learned more about his background. 'He was a native of this place' but since his trip away he said there were 'scarce any left alive besids him selfe'. Squanto claimed that the notorious slave-trading Englishman Captain Hunt, and first captured him and that he was lucky to escape at all because 'He was caried away with diverce others by one Hunt, a master of a ship, who thought to sell them for slaves in Spaine; but he got away for England, and was entertained by a marchante in London, & imployed to New-found-land & other parts, & lastly brought hither into these parts by one Mr. Dermer, a gentle-man imployed by Sr. Ferdinando Gorges & others, for discovery, & other designes in these parts'.

The explorer Dermer had played an important part in the development of the area according to Squanto who claimed to have been a great peacemaker in the past between Dermer and other Indians and 'that he made the peace betweene the salvages of these parts & the English; of which this plantation, as it is intimated, had the benefite'.

Following the visit of Dermer to New England, Bradford claimed that other English adventurers had been so inspired by the published accounts of Dermer's visit that they had advocated settling the Plymouth area long before the Pilgrim plans. Quoting from these published accounts which he had obtained himself Bradford wrote that Dermer sung the praises of the local area writing in his book 'that place from whence Squanto, or Tisquantem, was taken away; which in Cap: Smiths mape is called Plimoth: and I would that Plimoth had the like comodities. I would say that the first plantation might hear be seated, if ther come to the number of 50 persons, or upward. Otherwise at

Charlton, because ther the savages are lese to be feared'.

Dermer continued; 'The Pocanawkits, which live to the west of Plimoth, bear an inveterate malice to the English, and are of more streingth then all the savags from thence to Penobscote. There desire of revenge was occasioned by an English man, who having many of them on bord, made a great slaughter with their murderers & smale shot'.

Nevertheless, Dermer wrote, 'The soyle of the borders of this great bay, may be compared to most of the plantations which I have seen in Virginia wher groweth the best Tobaco' and in 'the botume of that great bay is store of Codd & basse, or mulett' and to the north 'Massachussets is about 9 leagues from Plimoth, & situate in the mids between both, is full of ilands & peninsules very fertill for the most parte'.

Bradford also learnt of another expedition in which Squanto had been involved with Captain Dermer where, on 'going a shore amongst the Indans to trad, as he used to doe, was betrayed & assaulted by them, & all his men slaine, but one that kept the boat; but him selfe gott abord very sore wounded, & they had cut of his head upon the cudy of his boat, had not the man reskued him with a sword'. Bradford concluded: 'By all which it may appeare how farr these people were from peace, and with what danger this plantation was begune, save as the powerfull hand of the Lord did protect them'.

The Indians for their part suspected the Pilgrims. Squanto confessed to Bradford that the Indians feared the Pilgrims had come to revenge an earlier European crew who had been shipwrecked with unfortunate consequences on the same shore. He told Bradford this was 'partly the reason why they kept aloofe & were so long before they came to the English. He said about 3 years before, a French-ship was cast away at Cap-Codd, but the men gott ashore, & saved their lives, and much of their victails, & other goods; but after the Indeans heard of it, they geathered togeather from these parts, and never left watching & dogging them till they got advantage, and kild them all but 3 or 4 which they kept, & sent from one Sachem to another, to make sporte with, and used them worse then slaves' and 'they conceived this ship was now come to revenge it'.

31 March   As the month of March drew to a close the Pilgrims looked back on their tragic death toll. Although most of the Pilgrims had died in January and February the losses in March had also been great. There were still sickly ones that would not recover. The fatalities had been a dreadful blow to the little community. Both of the main scribes, Bradford and Winslow, had lost their original wives in the New World, as had their military leader Captain Standish. The Company's treasurer, Christopher Martin, his wife, and other members of the household had all perished. Priscilla was the only surviving member of the Mullins family; as was Mary Chilton from her family. Nine of the young, single

111

men had died. In reviewing the sad body count Bradford wrote at this stage that of the 'hundred persons which came first over in this first ship together, the greater half died in the general mortality, and most of them in two or three months' time'.

Even then nobody knew exactly what disease had taken such a toll of them, although Bradford referred to the scurvy and others mentioned coughs and colds, pneumonia and other diseases. But as Bradford said 'The wanting of houses and other comforts', having arrived in the freezing New England winter, following months on the long voyage with an inferior diet, itself an ordeal, was enough to kill off all but the really fit'.

It had been a grim start for the new colony. During the worst moments the 'living were scarce able to bury the dead' and 'the well were not sufficient to tend the sick'. There were during their greatest illness 'but six or seven' able to move about to help others 'although they spared no pains to help them'.

But now with virtually half the company dead, it was time for them to stand alone. The *Mayflower* had to return to England.

1 April Bradford recounted that, although almost half the *Mayflower*'s crew of fifty had also died, the ship was now ready and able to return to England and report the terrible news: 'They now begane to dispatch the ship away which brought them over, which lay tille aboute this time and the reason on their parts why she stayed so long, was the necessitie and danger that lay upon them, for it was well towards the end of Desember before she could land any thing hear, or they able to receive any thing ashore'.

It must have been a frightening moment for those staying behind as the ship prepared to leave them in the new land with all its problems. Nevertheless Bradford said they would have liked the ship to have left earlier because of the extra cost of keeping the ship there. He explained however that the ship could not have sailed any earlier as they needed it as a safe base. In January, for example, 'the house which they had made for a generall randevoze by casulty fell afire, and some were faine to retire abord for shilter'.

'Then the sicknes begane to fall sore amongst them, and the weather so bad as they could not make much sooner any dispatch' and so 'seeing so many dye, and fall downe sick dayly, thought it no wisdom to send away the ship, their condition considered, and the danger they stood in from the Indeans, till they could procure some shelter; and therfore thought it better to draw some more charge upon them selves & freinds, then hazard all'.

Having delayed sailing and lost many crew, the *Mayflower* could not have returned until some of the sick sailors recovered: 'The master and sea-men like-wise, though before they hasted the passengers a shore to be goone, now many of their men being dead, & of the ablest of them, (as is before noted,) and of the rest many lay sick & weake, the master durst not put to sea, till he saw his men begine to receover, and the hart of winter over'.

So, the moment of parting came and the Pilgrims gathered on the beach to watch the *Mayflower* sail out into the Atlantic, thereby cutting their connection with England. It was one of the most dramatic moments since they had arrived and one that must have really tested the faint-hearted.

None of the Pilgrims however asked to go back with the ship, Bradford said; despite the appalling number of deaths they all remained committed to the mission.

3 April   The departure of the *Mayflower* might have been too much for the troublesome John Billington, however. Soon he opposed Captain Standish and refused to obey the military leader's lawful commands. Instead Billington began to hit out with 'opprobrious speeches' and had to be punished before he undermined the authority of his leaders.

The Pilgrims met and decided that anybody who challenged the authority of their military leader had to be disciplined or a dangerous precedent could be set.

4 April   The Pilgrims assembled and punished John Billington by tying him up with his neck and heels fastened together. As he was being tied up, however, Billington apologized and pleaded for mercy so they decided that, he could be forgiven, especially as it was a first offence.

Unfortunately, Billington continued to cause trouble and by the turn of the decade had murdered a fellow Pilgrim for which he had to be executed.

7 April   The Pilgrims continued to concentrate on growing their future food supplies with the help of Squanto: 'they (as many as were able) began to plant ther corne, in which servise Squanto stood them in great stead, showing them both the maner how to set it, and after how to dress & tend it'.

15 April   The planting proceeded well as the Pilgrims continued to learn new agricultural skills from Squanto.

Bradford described how Squanto was invaluable as a fishing and trapping expert as 'he tould them how to gett fish & set traps (in these old grounds)' and 'he showed them that in the midle of Aprill they should have store enough come up the brooke, by which they had begane to build, and taught them how to take it, and wher to get other provissions necessary for them; all which they found true by triall & experience'.

The Pilgrims were beginning to realize how many mistakes they had been making and how badly they needed Squanto's help in order to survive: 'Some English seed they sew, as wheat & pease, but it came not to good, eather by the badnes of the seed, or latenes of the season, or both, or some other defecte'.

21 April   As if all the deaths of the rank and file were not enough, tragedy again struck the little settlement when the popular Pilgrim leader was cut down by the insidious sickness that had eaten away at them from the start. Bradford said death struck during a warm spring day when most people were out in the fields: 'Whilst they were bussie about their seed, their Govr (Mr. John Carver) camne out of the feild very sick, it being a hott day; he complained greatly of his head, and lay downe, and within a few howers his sences failed'.

24 April   Although Doctor Fuller and others did all they could Governor Carver 'never spake more till he dyed' and 'his death was much lamented, and caused great heavines amongst them, as ther was cause'. With their religious leader John Robinson still in Leyden and their foundation Governor dead the Pilgrims could now have broken up as a group had it not been for their discipline and resolve.

25 April   Other men with initiative then organized a formal funeral with what pomp and ceremony could be mustered. Bradford said Governor Carver was then 'buried in the best maner they could, with some vollies of shott by all that bore armes'.

    After the sermon however a grim silence hung over the pathetic little community. Nobody's life seemed safe.

27 April   The Pilgrims assembled to select a new Governor.

    After some debate they selected the official scribe, William Bradford. In time Bradford turned out to be an excellent choice and was from then on re-elected year after year, even though he was not exactly fit and well himself at the time and needed a helper; he reported himself: 'William Bradford was chosen Governor in his stead, and being not yet recovered of his ilness, in which he had been near the point of death, Isaak Allerton was chosen to be an Asistante unto him, who, by renewed election every year, continued sundry years togeather, which I hear note once for all'.

It was important that the living continue to regroup and reproduce; Spring was celebrated with 'the first mariage in this place', Bradford said, when the widowed Winslow married Susanna White whose husband had died in February.

12 May   The wedding was a happy moment for the settlement and, being practical people, it 'was thought most requisite to be performed by the magistrate, as being a civill thing, upon which many questions about inheritances doe depende'.

2 July   With summer warming the settlement, the Pilgrims became more adventurous and planned to visit their neighbor and friend, Massasoit. Bradford, by now recovering, said: 'Haveing in some sorte ordered their bussines at home, it was thought meete to send some abroad to see their new friend Massasoyet, and to bestow upon him some gratiutie to bind him the faster unto them; as also that hearby they might view the countrie, and see in what maner he lived, what strength he had aboute him, and how the ways were to his place'.

Winslow said that they were going to 'Packanokik, the Habitation of the Great King Massasoyt', with a present for the Chief in the form of a a horseman's coat of red cotton laced with a slight lace which symbolized his desire that the peace and amity that was between them might be continued.

Bradford said that for this expedition, 'They sente Mr. Edward Winslow & Mr. Hopkins, with the foresaid Squanto for ther guid, who gave him a suite of cloaths, and a horsemans coate, with some other small things, which were kindly accepted; but they found but short commons, and came both weary & hungrie home. For the Indeans used then to have nothing'.

On their inland expedition Winslow and Hopkins saw many 'amazing' things. They 'found his place to be 40 miles from hence, the soyle good, & the people not many, being dead & abundantly wasted in the late great mortalitie which fell in all these parts aboute three years before the coming of the English, wherin thousands of them dyed, they not being able to burie one another; ther sculs and bones were found in many places lying still above ground, where their houses & dwellings had been; a very sad spectackle to behould'.

As the Pilgrims were now short of food, Winslow told Massasoit they could no longer give his Indians such entertainment as they had done in the past. And to establish a messenger system they suggested that in future all official messengers carried a copper chain.

The Pilgrims also asked for trading goods to send back to England, such as skins — and if the Indians had any spare corn they would exchange some of their corn for seed.

Winslow described how he and Hopkins met some ten or twelve men women and children on route to Massasoit's village, who pestered them till they were weary of them. About three o'clock in the afternoon the Indians entertained them in the best manner they could, giving them a kind of bread. After the meal the Indians desired one of the Pilgrims to shoot at a crow complaining what damage they sustained in their corn by them. When the Pilgrims shot some 'fourscore off' the Indians were very impressed.

3 July   Winslow described how the next morning they had breakfast, took their leave and departed accompanied by six savages. Finally they reached a riverside and found they had to wade through. Winslow was impressed by the courage of two elderly Indians on the opposite side of the river. He said these two men were both aged especially one who was 'above three score'; nevertheless on spotting the Winslow group entering the river, they ran very swiftly and low in the grass to meet the Pilgrims at the bank where, with shrill voices, they charged at them, no doubt supposing them to be enemies and thinking to take advantage while they were in the water. But seeing the Pilgrims were friends, they welcomed them with such food as they had and the Pilgrims gave them a small bracelet of beads in return.

The Indians 'proved' friendly, Winslow recalled. Whenever the Pilgrims came to any small brook, their Indian companions would offer to carry them across. They offered to carry their goods when the Pilgrims looked weary. Even when Winslow or Hopkins took off a bit of clothing, they wanted to carry it.

Eventually they reached the village of Massasoit but he was not at home. Massasoit was sent for. During their wait, one of the Pilgrims unintentionally upset the local people. Just by picking up his gun, he caused the women and children to run away; they thought he was about to shoot them. Indeed, they could not be pacified till he laid it down again.

4 July   When the Indian Chief returned, he gave Winslow and Hopkins a welcome equal to that Governor Carver had given him back in Plymouth.

Winslow described how the Pilgrims greeted Massasoit by firing off their guns in a salute and then he kindly welcomed the Pilgrims, and took them into his house. Once they had delivered their message and presents and had bedecked him with the coat and the chain, Massasoit strutted around proudly so his people could behold him.

These follow-up negotiations were also a success. Massasoit affirmed that he would gladly continue the peace and friendship. He then made a great speech with other Indians sometimes interposing, by way of either confirming or applauding him in what he said. Winslow complained that, although for the Indians the speech might have been 'delightful', the Pilgrims found it very tedious.

Massasoit ended his speech after he expressed loyalty to the English King and told the Pilgrims he felt sorry for King James whose wife Queen Anne had died in 1619. He then lit tobacco for them and fell to discoursing about England and marvelling that the King would live without a wife.

The two Pilgrims spent that night with the Chief, curled up on the same bed with Massasoit and his wife; they at one end, and the Pilgrims at the other. The bed was only planks laid a foot above the ground with a thin mat upon it. Two other tribal leaders also pressed in to sleep there, so that by morning Winslow complained they were more weary 'of their lodging, than of their journey'.

5 July Winslow and Hopkins were now anxious to return but Massasoit wanted to have them stay with him longer. Winslow told him the Pilgrims desired to keep the Sabbath at home; and feared they should be lightheaded for want of sleep. For what with bad lodging, the Indians' 'barbarous' singing, the lice and fleas and mosquitoes, the Pilgrims could hardly get any sleep at all.

6 July A rather tired Winslow said that before sunrise they took their leave and departed. Six Indians insisted on accompanying them.

Despite the exhaustive nature of the expedition and a 'great' storm they had to endure on the return journey, the Winslow–Hopkins expedition proved highly successful. They arrived back at the settlement wet and extremely weary, but at least they had returned safely from their venture into the unknown.

21 July Although Winslow and Hopkins had demonstrated that the Pilgrims could venture into the woods and return safely, others still got lost, especially when they failed to take a guide. Bradford said that John Billington Junior, the son of the difficult John Billington (who had earlier challenged Captain Standish), now caused trouble when he disappeared 'and lost him selfe in the woods, & wandered up & down some 5 days, living on beries & what he could find. At length he light on an Indean plantation, 20 miles south of this place, called Manamet, they conveid him furder off, to Nawsett, among those people that had before set upon the English when they were coasting, whilest the ship lay at the Cape, as was before noted'.

Young Billington could have been killed by this hostile tribe, Bradford said, 'But the Gover caused him to be enquired for among the Indeans' and 'at length Massassoyt sent word wher he was, and the Gover sent a shalop for him, & had him delivered'.

This rescue party with Squanto in assistance nevertheless had problems. Winslow said ten of their men went to find the boy, but before they had been long at sea a storm of wind and rain blew up, with much lightning and thunder. They also got a fright when a 'spout' of water rose not far from them, so they put in that night at Barnstable Harbor. In the morning, they met some 'savages' who agreed to take the Pilgrims to young Billington. Winslow said the boy was apparently well but, as he was still some distance off at Nauset, the Indians invited them to come ashore and eat with them. So they sent six ashore and left four on guard in the boat.

Winslow said that after sunset the Chief, Aspinet, came with a great train bringing the boy with him, one Indian bearing him through the

After the first long winter the Pilgrims were grateful for the spring that brought life back to Cape Cod Harbor.

water. The Chief had not less than a hundred braves with him. There Aspinet delivered the boy to them, dressed up with beads. He made peace with the Pilgrims and departed.

In return for this tribe's generosity, Bradford related how the Pilgrims went down to their area and gave them back the same amount of corn as that which the Pilgrims had taken from them on first arriving in the Cape Cod area: 'Those people also came and made their peace; and they gave full satisfaction to those whose corne they had found & taken when they were at Cap-Codd'.

On this expedition the rescue party had come across a very old Indian lady who had wanted to meet English people ever since her sons had been kidnapped by the dreaded slave trader Captain Hunt. Winslow explained that the one thing which had been 'very grievous' for them on this trip was the meeting with a woman, whom they judged to be no less than a hundred years old. Winslow said she came to see them because she had never seen English people yet could not set eyes on them without breaking 'forth into great passion, weeping and crying excessively'. It turned out she had three sons, who, when Master Hunt was in these parts, went aboard his ship to trade with him. Hunt kidnapped them and carried them off as slaves to Spain.

Rumors of Indian attack against the settlement in their absence then struck fear into the rescue party, especially as they knew the colony was so weakly guarded. Excluding these ten men, there were now only twenty-two adult males at Plymouth. So they set off to return home with as much haste as they could. Despite having to put in again to shore because the wind was 'contrary' and having to make their way back in the dark, they reached Plymouth that night.

But there had been no attack, and Bradford wrote: 'Thus ther peace & aquaintance was prety well establlisht with the native aboute them'. In fact, the Pilgrims had been busy making new friends; Bradford: 'ther was an other Indean called Hobamack come to live amongst them, a proper lustie man, and a man of acconte for his vallour & parts amongst the Indeans, and continued very faithfull and constant to the English till he dyed'.

13 August There continued to be false alarms however. On this day, the Indian Hobamack came running to them with the story that Squanto had been taken, and possibly murdered, by another Chief, called Corbitant. Bradford wrote: 'He & Squanto being gone upon bussines amonge the Indeans, at their returne (whether it was out of envie to them or malice to the English) ther was a Sachem called Corbitant, alyed to Massassoyte, but never any good freind to the English to this day, mett with them at an Indean towne caled Namassakett 14 miles to the west of this place, and begane to quarell with them, and offered to stab Hobamack; but being a lusty man, he cleared him selfe of him, and came running away all sweating and tould the Govr what had befalne him, and he feared they had killed Squanto, for they threatended them

118

both, and for no other cause but because they were freinds to the English, and servisable unto them'. It sounded a serious situation, so Bradford discussed it with the other Pilgrim leaders.

14 August

Bradford continued: 'Upon this the Governor taking counsell, it was conceivd not fitt to be borne; for it they should suffer their freinds & messengers thus to be wronged, they should have none would cleave unto them, or give them any inteligence, or doe them serviss afterwards; but nexte they would fall upon them selves. Whereupon it was resolved to send the Captaine & 14 men well armed, and to goe & fall upon them in the night; and if they found that Squanto was kild, to cut of Corbitants head, but not to hurt any but those that had a hand it it. Hobamack was asked if he would goe & be their guide, & bring them ther before day. He said he would, & bring them to the house wher the man lay, and show them which was he'.

A military party was then mounted, Winslow said, to journey to the 'Kingdom of Namaschet', to revenge the supposed death of their interpreter Squanto. At Namaschet, they charged the 'house of Corbitant' and demanded to see him. According to Bradford, they: 'beset the house round; the Captin giving charg to let none pass out, entred the house to search for him. But he was goone away that day, so they mist him; but understood that Squanto was alive, & that he had only threatened to kill him, & made an offer to stab him but did not. So they withheld and did no more hurte, & the people came trembling, & brought them the best provissions they had'.

In the end, a fight did not eventuate. Winslow said the Indians told them that Squanto was still living and set about offering the Pilgrims some tobacco and food. The Pilgrims refused and were searching the house when Hobamack returned Squanto alive, before fleeing himself.

The Pilgrims took away all the bows and arrows they could find, promising to return them in the morning. They remained in the house that night, but released the Indians they had taken captive.

15th August

Winslow says that next morning, they marched into the midst of the 'town'; and went to the house of Squanto to breakfast. The Pilgrims had done well, Winslow thought, for, although Corbitant had escaped, he now realized there was no place he could hide for long if he continued threatening them. As for those who were wounded, the Pilgrims offered to take them back to Plymouth where Surgeon Samuel Fuller could treat them. The party returned safety home that night.

This false alarm and the Pilgrim reaction laid the groundwork for better relations with the Indians in the future: 'After this they had many congratulations from diverce Chiefs, and much firmer peace; yea, those of the Iles of Capawack sent to make frendship; and this Corbitant him selfe used the mediation of Massassoyte to make his peace, but was shie to come neare them a long while after'.

18 September   The Pilgrims now became much more adventurous. They had decided that it was time to make friends with the traditionally hostile tribe to the north. Winslow said they now set out in the shallop on a voyage to the Massachusetts, which was partly to see the country and partly to make peace with the northern Indian tribes. To make a good start on the best tide they set out about midnight from Plymouth to cover the forty miles to the Boston location of the Indians.

19 September   Having rowed and sailed for some time they reached their destination of Boston Harbor, Winslow said, but being late they anchored and lay in the shallop, not having sighted any of the local Indians.

20 September   With the daylight, Winslow said, they put in for the shore, and Captain Myles Standish and four of their company went to seek the local chief to 'enlist' him as a friend.

Once the Pilgrims met the chief, named Obbattinnua, they tried to persuade him to swear allegiance to the English King by telling him of the different Indian Chiefs who had already acknowledged themselves to be King James's men. They promised to protect him from his enemies if he would do so. Finally Obbattinnua agreed.

The Pilgrims returned to their boat and, to be safe from attack that night, they rode at anchor aboard the shallop.

21 September   Next day, the Pilgrims then went exploring and looking for other friendly Indians. Winslow recorded that they went ashore at Squantum, Dorchester and marched, in arms, up country until they came to a place where corn had been newly gathered, and a house pulled down. This was near Milton Hill.

Much to their surprise this 'house' turned out to be a kind of tomb within a 'Fort'. It consisted of a blockade with a diameter of about forty or fifty feet made of poles some thirty or forty feet high. There was a surrounding trench, 'breast high', and only one entrance across a bridge. In the center of this stood the frame of a house and inside a body lay buried.

Within a mile of here, they found a group of Indian women. Winslow said that initially the women were afraid of them, but then seeing their 'gentle carriage' towards them, they took heart and entertained the Pilgrims in the 'best manner' they could, even cooking cod for them. Finally, they told the Pilgrims that the tomb belonged to Chief Nanepashemet who was struck down by the plague and that his widow now ruled the area.

At length one of their men came forward, 'shaking and trembling for fear'. Winslow said they asked to see this Indian 'Queen' but he claimed she was far away. At this point Squanto 'showed his savage instincts', as he wanted the Pilgrims to steal all the skins and suchlike that might be useful; he said they were a 'bad' people who have often threatened the Pilgrims.

Winslow wrote that the Pilgrims refused to 'wrong them', or give the Indians any reason to revenge. He also commented on the modesty of the Indian women who 'hid' their bodies from them. When they returned to the shallop, almost all the women accompanied them to trade. And although the women sold their coats from their backs and 'tied boughs about them', they did so with 'great shamefastness'.

It was during this reprisal expedition that the Pilgrims found useful sea lanes. Indeed, Winslow considered that these more northern areas were better harbors for shipping and offered greater potential for survival as, although most of the islands had been inhabited, the local Indians were all dead, or 'removed', due to the plague.

22 September The expedition returned safely home before noon: 'They returned in saftie, and brought home a good quanty of beaver, and made reporte of the place, wishing they had been ther seated; (but it seems the Lord, who assignes to all men the bounds of their habitations, had apoynted it for an other use)'.

With the summer now ended, it was time to take stock of their situation. If the crops were successful and their other food gathering effort proved effective they could survive a second winter; if not they might all die.

The Pilgrims had worked hard, conditions had been kind to them and they appeared to be in a good position to survive. Bradford wrote: 'They begane now to gather in the small harvest they had, and to fitte up their houses and dwellings against winter, being all well recovered in health & strength and had all things in good plenty, for as some were thus imployed in affairs abroad, others were exersised in fishing, aboute codd, & bass, & other fish, of which they tooke good store, of which every family had their portion'.

Those that had survived the winter of death had in fact been treated to a summer of great plenty. The plentiful fish, birds and other animals had all added to the crop produce making this in many ways the promised land they had been seeking. Bradford claimed: 'All the sommer ther was no wante. And now begane to come in store of foule, as winter approached, of which this place did abound when they came first (but afterward decreased by degrees). And besids water foule, ther was great store of wild Turkies, of which they tooke many, besids vension, &c. Besids they had about a peck a meale a weeke to a person, or now since harvest, Indean corne to that proportion. Which made many afterwards write so largly of their plenty hear to their friends in England, which were not fained, but true reports'.

Winslow also confirmed that the crops were good. He said in the first spring they had planted some twenty acres of Indian corn, sowed some six acres of barley and pease and, in the manner of Indians, manured their ground with 'herrings and shads', in great abundance and found with great ease at their doors. Their seeds turned out well and God be praised, he said, they had a 'good increase' of Indian Corn.

| **The First Thanksgiving** | Because the New World had been so kind to them, the Pilgrims then decided to give thanks to God for their produce and to the local Indians who had helped them by organizing a major feast. |

The most honored guest of all was, of course, Massasoit and his fellow braves and their squaws. For three days, the Pilgrims entertained and feasted. The Indians killed five deer which they brought back to the Plantation and 'bestowed' on their hosts.

9 November

They had not seen any sign of a sailing ship for over a year by now. Consequently, the Pilgrims were besides themselves with joy when suddenly over the horizon a set of white sails appeared.

After hearing the warning from their lookout, they rushed to the beach to discover that this ship was the *Fortune*. Eager for news, they were reassured by the people who struggled ashore from their long boats that the *Mayflower* had sailed safely back to England. Now the *Fortune* had brought a second party of settlers.

This was the biggest milestone in their experiment so far. The settlement was being taken seriously back in England and, with new laborers and breeders, it could now succeed. Having feared that they might all perish, it now seemed they could survive a second winter.

The *Fortune* had sailed direct from England with thirty-five passengers for the Plymouth Plantation. It arrived on 9 November and Bradford observed that this was 'about that time twelfe month that them selves came'. The Pilgrims were surprised, it was a 'small ship to them unexpected or loked for'.

The numbers in Plymouth had swelled suddenly from less than fifty to eighty-five. In fact, by morning it had become eighty-six, as the 'goodwife' Ford gave birth to a son the first night she landed.

The new batch of settlers included Robert Cushman, their old Pilgrim friend, who had remained with the abandoned *Speedwell* when they had set out from England in August 1620: 'the *Fortune* contained Mr. Cushman (so much spoken of before) and with him 35 persons to remaine & live in the plantation; which did not a litle rejoyce them'.

The new arrivals were relieved to find the Pilgrim settlement flourishing as many had begun to doubt the viability of the new plantation: 'And they when they came a shore and found all well, and saw plenty of vitails in every house, were no less glade. For most of them were lusty yonge men, and many of them wild enough, who litle considered whither or aboute what they wente, till they came into the harbore at Cap-Codd, and ther saw nothing but a naked and barren place'.

In fact, the new settlers had been so worried that the Pilgrims had not made a good start that they stole the sails from the yards to stop the *Fortune* leaving without them if they decided not to stay. Bradford said the newcomers on the *Fortune* 'then begane to thinke what should become of them, if the people here were dead or cut of by the Indeans.

They begane to consulte (upon some speeches that some of the sea-men had cast out) to take the sayls from the yeard least the ship should gett away and leave them ther'.

'But the master hereing of it, gave them good words, and tould them if any thing but well should have befallne the people hear, he hoped he had vitals enough to cary them to Virginia, and whilst he had a bitt they should have their parte; which gave them good satisfaction'.

Then the reality of the situation suddenly dawned on the Plymouth Pilgrims: the second group of settlers had arrived totally empty-handed! Although they themselves were still worried about having enough food to last them through the coming winter, the new arrivals had not had the good sense to bring any food or supplies. Bradford said with some amazement: 'So they were all landed; but ther was not so much as bisket-cake or any other victialls. (Nay, they were faine to spare the shipe some to carry her home) for them'.

Furthermore, they found out that the new group had not even brought equipment such as beds, kitchen utensils or clothing to this virgin and empty land. Bradford said 'neither had they any beding, but some sory things they had in their cabins, not pot, nor pan, to drese any meate in; nor overmany cloaths, for many of them had brusht away their coats & cloaks at Plimoth as they came'. It was a potential disaster. Fortunately as far as the clothes went Bradford said they found some substitutes on the ship, as 'ther was sent over some burching-lane suits in the ship, out of which they were supplied'.

In all, 'the plantation was glad of this addition of strength, but could have wished that many of them had been of beter condition, and all of them beter furnished with provissions; but that could not now be helpte'.

The situation was not helped by the news from home either. The main letter was from the disgruntled agent Weston who had already exploited them with such unreasonable investors' contracts. Bradford said 'In this ship Mr. Weston sent a large leter to Mr. Carver, the late Govenor, now deseased, full of complaints'.

The impatient investors were unhappy with the returns on their capital outlay and were very angry that the Pilgrims had not sent more trading goods back with the *Mayflower*. Weston argued that he was still on the side of the Pilgrims because he had pretended that things were better in Plymouth than they really were to stop the investors pulling out of the venture, especially after it had lost half its labor force. Weston confided to the Pilgrims 'had they knowne as much as I doe, they would not have adventured a halfe-peny of what was necessary for this ship'.

He professed that he could not believe that the returning *Mayflower* had not been loaded up with beaver furs and other goods for sale in London: 'That you sent no lading in the ship is wonderfull, and worthily distated. I know your weaknes was the cause of it, and I beleeve more

By the spring the Pilgrims were finding ample game to supplement their meagre rations.

weaknes of judgmente, then weaknes of hands. A quarter of the time you spente in discoursing, arguing, & consulting, would have done much more'.

Weston then gave them a final warning. If the remaining Pilgrims did not sign a copy of the original contract and send it back, promising to do better in future, along with an account of how they had spent their money so far, he would not help them any more: 'If you mean, bona fide, to performe the conditions agreed upon, doe us the favore to coppy them out faire, and subscribe them with the principall of your names. And likwise give us accounte as perticulerly as you can how our moneys were laid out'.

Most of all Weston demanded they fill up the *Fortune* with riches for her return journey warning them that otherwise the investors would demand repayment of their initial capital outlay, 'And consider that the life of the bussines depends on the lading of this ship, which, if you doe to any good purpose'.

Bradford replied on behalf of the dead Governor Carver and other Pilgrims: 'You lay many heavie imputations upon him and us all'. Bradford said of Carver, 'He needs not my appologie; for his care and pains was so great for the commone good, both ours and yours and he oppressed him selfe and shortened his days'. Bradford said he was aware of the great cost to the adverturers and even the losses they may sustain; however 'the loss of his and many other honest and industrious mens lives, cannot be vallewed at any prise'.

Bradford was hurt that Weston had wanted the *Mayflower* back earlier, and so defended his Pilgrim party when he wrote in reply: 'You greatly blame us for keping the ship so long in the countrie, and then to send her away emptie. She lay 5 weks at Cap-Codd, whilst with many a weary step (after a long journey) and the indurance of many a hard brunte, we sought out in the foule winter a place of habitation. Then we went in so tedious a time to make provission to sheelter us and our goods'.

He tried to justify the failure to supply the investors with trading goods saying it 'pleased God to vissite us then, with death dayly, and with so generall a disease, that the living were scarce able to burie the dead; and the well not in any measure sufficente to tend the sick. And now to be so greatly blamed, for not fraighting the ship, doth indeed goe near us, and much discourage us. But you say you know we will pretend weaknes; and doe you think we had not cause?'

With the letter so answered, the Pilgrims turned their attention to assimilating the new arrivals and getting the ship back to England as instructed by Weston — this time with worthwhile exports. Bradford: 'This ship (caled the Fortune) was speedily dispatcht away, being laden with good clapboard as full as she could stowe, and 2 hoggsheads of beaver and otter skins, which they gott with a few trifling comodities brought with them at first, being alltogeather unprovided for trade'.

Bradford did not think it was fair to expect the Pilgrims to be good fur traders as 'neither was ther any amongst them that ever saw a beaver skin till they came hear, and were informed by Squanto'. Nevertheless the Pilgrims had done their best; Bradford said 'The fraight was estimated to be worth near £500'.

According to Bradford, it also turned out that Cushman had come to interview the Pilgrims for the investors: 'Mr. Cushman returned backe also with this ship, for so Mr. Weston & the rest had apoynted him, for their better information. And he doubted not, nor them selves neither, but they should have a speedy supply'.

23 November The Pilgrim settlement was now moving into a new and more difficult stage.

Bradford wrote: 'After the departure of this ship, (which stayed not above 14 days,) the Govr & his assistante haveing disposed these late commers into severall families, as they best could, tooke an exacte accounte of all their provissions in store, and proportioned the same to the number of persons'.

Having done the calculations of people and food supplies Bradford announced that he had 'found that it would not hould out above 6 months at halfe alowance, and hardly that. And they could not well give less this winter time till fish came in againe'. There was only one alternative — to cut the ration: 'So they were presently put to half alowance, one as well as an other, which begane to be hard, but they bore it patiently under hope of supply'.

The shortages of food and other supplies were not going to be made any easier by a sudden change in relations with the Indians. The arrival of the *Fortune* inspired the Indians to protest at all these extra numbers coming to occupy their land. At any moment a fight could break out, and the Pilgrims began to worry once more about an Indian attack. Winslow explained that the great people of Nanohigganset which were reported to be many thousands strong began to 'breathe forth many' threats against the Pilgrims. Suddenly there was Indians on all sides and, although the Pilgrims had extra numbers now, those from the *Fortune* had brought no arms at all. It was a dangerous situation.

The Indians brought the situation to a head when, as Bradford reported: 'Sone after this ships departure, the great people of the Narigansets, in a braving maner, sente a messenger unto them with a bundl of arrows tyed aboute with a great sneak-skine; which their interpretours tould them was a threatening & a chaleng'. Leaving, a bundle of new arrows wrapped in a rattlesnake's skin was a great insult. The Indians had thrown down the gauntlet and the age of serious conflict had arrived.

Bradford responded: 'With the advice of others, we thus sente them a round answere, that if they had rather have warre then peace, they might begine when they would; we had done them no wrong, neither did they fear them, or should they find they unprovided'.

In order to demonstrate a show of strength, the Pilgrims bravely replied with a similar gesture. After some deliberation, the Governor stuffed the rattlesnake's skin with powder and shot; and sent it back. 'It was no small terror to this savage King, insomuch as he would not once touch the powder and shot, or suffer it to stay in his house or country: whereupon, the messenger refusing it, another took it up; and having been posted from place to place a long time, at length came whole back again to Plymouth'.

With so many more people to protect, the Pilgrims would have to build a bigger fort. This was now a new era in their history. Bradford wrote: 'But this made them the more carefully to looke to them selves, so as they agreed to inclose their dwellings with a good strong pale, and make flankers in convenient places, with gates to shute, which were every night locked, and a watch kept, and when neede required ther was also warding in the day time'.

They also increased the emergency military drill. 'The company was by the Captaine and the Govr advise, devided into 4 squadrons, and every one had ther quarter apoynted them, unto which they were to repaire upon any suddane alarme. And if ther should be any crie of fire, a company were appointed for a gard, with muskets, whilst others quenchet the same, to prevent Indean treachery. This was accomplished very cherfully'. Bradford added that the town was 'impayled round by the begining of March, in which evry family had a prety garden plote secured'.

With this entry, Bradford concluded: 'And herewith I shall end this year.'

The end of the year 1621 ushered in the second stage of the Pilgrim story. The people who were to act out this drama were those in the second wave who had arrived on the *Fortune*; the success or failure of the settlement would depend greatly on their performance. Bradford and the original 102 Pilgrim settlers had established the foothold but there was still much work to be done.

As these new settlers were so vital to the future of this founding American settlement it is fitting to end this account of the birth of the colony with a list of the 'second comers' recorded as on board the *Fortune*.

The *Fortune* Pilgrims

1. John Adams, carpenter from London.
2. William Bassett, gunsmith and metal worker, Bethnal Green, London.
3. William Beale.
4. Edward Bompasse, from London, one of the 'lusty yonge men'.
5. Jonathan Brewster, ribbon maker, son of William Brewster the Elder from Scrooby.
6. Clement Brigges, fellmonger from Southward, Surrey.

7. John Cannon, bachelor from London.
8. William Coner, Bachelor.
9. Robert Cushman, wool carder and agent, who came for observation only and returned to England with the *Fortune*.
10. Thomas Cushman.
11. Stephen Dean, miller, bachelor, another of the 'lusty yonge men'.
12. Phillipe de la Noye, sixteen years of age when he arrived, probably a servant to one of the other passengers.
13. Thomas Flavel, probably from one of the suburbs of London, with Master Flavel, his son.
14. Master Ford, first name unknown, husband of Martha Ford.
15. Martha Ford, who was delivered of a son the first night she landed.
16. Robert Hicks, fellmonger of London.
17. William Hilton, possibly fishmonger, of Northwich, Chester.
18. Benedict Morgan, sailor, of Clerkenwell, London, returned to England in the *Anne*
19. Thomas Morton, possibly from Austerfield, York, home of Bradford.
20. Austin Nicolas, may have been of Flemish origin.
21. William Palmer, nailer, one of the older passengers, possibly from London.
22. William Pitt, probably returned to England prior to 1627.
23. Thomas Prence, future Governor, had just reached majority when he emigrated.
24. Moses Simonson, possibly a minor when he emigrated, member of the Church at Leyden.
25. Hugh Statie, a yeoman, not a freeman until 1642 may have been brought over as an apprentice by one of the other passengers.
26. James Steward, no further record of him at Plymouth after 1623.
27. William Tench, very little known.
28. John Winslow, brother of Edward, passenger on the *Mayflower*, from Worcester, England.
29. William Wright, married Priscilla Carpenter, was one of the older passengers, possibly connected with the Leyden congregation.

25 December The likely success or failure of the settlement was soon indicated in a final incident recorded on Christmas Day by the tireless Governor Bradford. He was one of the old guard who believed that from the way the newcomers behaved on such an important day there would be tensions in the future and he said by way of conclusion: 'Only I shall remember one passage more, rather of mirth then of waight. On the day called Chrismas-day, the Govenor caled them out to worke, (as was usual,) but the most of this new-company excused them selves and said it wente against their consciences to work on that day. So the Govenor tould them that if they made it mater of conscience, he would spare them till they were better informed.

'So he led-away the rest and left them; but when they came home at noone from their worke, he found them in the streete at play, openly; some pitching the barr, & some at stoole-ball, and shuch like sports. So he went to them, and tooke away their implements, and tould them that was against his conscience, that they should play & others worke. If they made the keeping of it mater of devotion, let them kepe their houses, but ther should be no gameing or revelling in the streets. Since which time nothing hath been attempted that way, at least openly'.

This incident marked a turning point. The initial period of the united and disciplined puritan colony had come to an end. From now on, the innocence of 'the first comers' — the early Pilgrim Fathers — would never be recaptured and tensions and divisions would mark the developing settlement in the New World.

The Pilgrims had succeeded in planting their religious seed in North America against all odds but the society that was to grow from this early beginning became vastly different to the one they had dreamed of.

Postscript:
The Founding of America

*It was to the admiration of many, and
allmost wonder of the world; that of so
small beginnings so great things should
insue, as time after manifested; and that
here should be such a resting place for so
many of the Lords people, when so sharp
a scourge came upon their owne nation*
William Bradford

The Pilgrims survived the second winter, despite the thirty-five extra mouths to feed and enjoyed an even better harvest in the spring of 1622. The *Fortune* managed to get back to England, although French pirates highjacked the vessel on the way and stole most of the goods. The London investors had to be kept happy by the promises from the Pilgrims that other ships would take lucrative cargoes back to England in future years.

The Plymouth Plantation grew from a population of eighty-five in 1621, as more and more Pilgrim settlers arrived. Ships like the *Anne* and the *Little James* arrived within a year and by 1623 the bulk of the original Leyden congregation sailed into Plymouth Harbor, reuniting many families. This was a most emotional moment as all the original Pilgrims were now together in the Promised Land.

Bradford sums up the feelings when he reports that 'These passengers, when they saw their low & poore condition a shore, were much daunted and dismayed, and according to their divers humores were diversly affected; some wished them selves in England againe; others fell a weeping, fancying their own miserie in what they saw now in others; other some pitying the distress they saw their freinds had been long in, and still were under; in a word, all were full of sadnes'.

Bradford married again and continued as Governor but, as the years went by, his job became more difficult. The new settlers were not always as well behaved as 'the first comers'.

Some of the more rebellious settlers even had to be expelled from the settlement. This proved counterproductive however because the rebels set up alternative 'pleasure camps' where other rebels could

Once the settlement had become established the Pilgrims were able to build substantial houses in Plymouth.

drink and dance and make love to Indian wenches.

This debauched behavior, which peaked some years later at the Merry Mount Maypole affair, eventually had to be suppressed by a punitive raid under Captain Standish in order to re-establish the original discipline of the Pilgrims. The Merry Mount affair started, Bradford tells us, when Thomas Morton, a well educated but unscrupulous adventurer, arrived and took control of a nearby plantation at Mount Wallarton. The pleasure-loving Morton immediately changed the name of the location to Merry Mount and began to plan some fun.

Bradford claimed that 'after this they all fell to a great licientiousness, and from then on led a most dissolute life'. Before long, Morton had become 'lord of misrule, and maintained (as it were) a school of sin. They set up a may-pole with much drinking, dancing and consorting with the Indian women'. Then to make matters worse the pleasure seekers were forced to trade their guns, powder and shot in return for food from the Indians in order to maintain their abandoned lifestyle.

At this point the Pilgrims lost patience as not only was this pleasure camp undermining their puritan values but with arms and ammunition the Indians would become more of a threat. Having tried in vain to persuade Morton to reform his ways, the Pilgrims eventually decided to storm the pleasure camp and take Morton and his revellers by force. Sending Captain Standish and a raiding party fully armed into the camp, the Pilgrims caught Morton and his men unawares, disarmed them, tied them up and dispatched Morton back to England on the next ship.

Although it was a victory for the way of life advocated by the Pilgrims it was not without some price. Once back in England, Morton published a book attacking the Pilgrims for their dictatorial methods.

By the end of the first decade, however, Pilgrim publications like *Mourt's Relation* and Winslow's *Good News from New England* had inspired other religious groups to cross the Atlantic and to share in the resources of the New World. By 1630 large shiploads of puritans under the leadership of Governor John Winthrop established other settlements in the Massachusetts Bay area which came under the auspices of the powerful Massachusetts Bay Company.

Before long the different settlements were forced to create a Federation in order to work together and to defeat the common Indian enemy as by then, with Squanto and Samoset long dead, the Indians opposed such massive numbers invading their country.

Then in 1643 the New England Confederation was created out of the four colonies of Massachusetts Bay, Connecticut, New Haven and Plymouth basically for defence against Indians, French and Dutch rivals in New England. The New England Confederation was the first union of independent colonies and was a model for the later Articles of Confederation, which led in turn to the Union of the United States.

Indeed as Bradford said himself 'it was to the admiration of many, and allmost wonder of the world; that of so small beginnings so great things should insue' ... 'So the light here kindled hath shone to many'.

Acknowledgments

This book could not have been written if not for the detailed records left by William Bradford, the official scribe of the Pilgrim mission. His journal tells the story from the persecution of the Pilgrims in England, right through the voyage of the *Mayflower* to the successful creation of Plymouth Plantation. It is beautifully-written, erudite, compassionate, and comprehensive — and without it there would be no comprehensive account available. The journal of Edward Winslow also provided many useful details, used in this reconstruction.

The people of Plymouth, Massachusetts, were all very cooperative on this project, from the first visit by the author in 1973 to the last research trip in 1985. Pilgrim Hall officials were extremely helpful; they included Laurence Pizer, Eleanor Driver and Caroline Chapin. The General Society of Mayflower Descendants was also most helpful, especially Barbara Merrick and her office staff. The Plymouth Research Officer, Timothy Taylor, was invaluable from start to finish and, as the man on the spot, made the book happen. The modern day Pilgrims at Plymouth Plantation and on board the *Mayflower* also provided the author with a lot of feeling for the period. The Plymouth Wax Museum was also helpful in creating atmosphere for the story, while in Holland, Dr. Jeremy Bangs provided helpful information from the Leyden Pilgrim Document Center.

Photo credits
The author wishes to thank Pilgrim Hall, the General Society of Mayflower Descendents and Plymouth Plantation for their kind permission to reproduce illustrations in this book. The author also wishes to thank those other organizations who so kindly gave permission to reproduce illustrations, including G. P. Putman & Sons, New York, and Jonathan Cape, London.

The Australian National Library provided first-class reference material through the assistance of Christine Bell. The Melbourne University Interlibrary loan staff, especially Christine Watts, provided additional reference material, while Monash University's Hazel Hunter also helped. Working from the journals, Janette Muddle typed the manuscript while my wife Jane King provided her usual back-up services.

Many thanks to you all.

Illustrations
The illustrations in this book come from a variety of sources including:
1. Pilgrim Hall collection, Plymouth, Mass., USA
2. General Society of Mayflower Descendants, Plymouth, Mass., USA
3. Plymouth Plantation, Mass., USA
4. William Bradford's *History of Plimouth Plantation*, Wright & Potter Printing Co., State Printers, Boston, Mass. 1898.
5. W. H. Bartlett, *The Pilgrim Fathers of New England*, Arthur Hall Cirtue & Co. London, 1853.
6. George Cheever, *The Pilgrim Fathers or the Journey of the Pilgrims*, William Collins, London, 1840.
7. Azel, Ames, *The Mayflower and her Log*, Houghton Mifflin & Company, Boston, 1901.
8. John Brown, *The Pilgrim Fathers of New England and their Puritan Successors*, The Religious Tract Society, London, 1897.
9. Mary Crawford, *In the days of the Pilgrim Fathers*, Little & Brown, Boston, 1920.
10. John Langdon Davies, *The Mayflower and the Pilgrim Fathers — a collection of contemporary documents*, Jackdaw #8, Jonathan Cape, London, 1965.
11. Leonard Cowie, *The Pilgrim Fathers*, G. P. Putnam & Sons, New York, 1972.

Index